Stairs

Stairs

Second edition

Alan and Sylvia Blanc

Architectural Press

OXFORD   AUCKLAND   BOSTON   JOHANNESBURG   MELBOURNE   NEW DELHI

Architectural Press
An imprint of Butterworth-Heinemann
Linacre House, Jordan Hill, Oxford OX2 8DP
225 Wildwood Avenue, Woburn, MA 01801-2041
A division of Reed Educational and Professional Publishing Ltd

Ɋ A member of the Reed Elsevier plc group

First published 1996
Second edition 2001

© Reed Educational and Professional Publishing Ltd 1996, 2001

British Library Cataloguing in Publication Data
Blanc, Sylvia
    Stairs. – 2nd ed.
    1. Staircases   2. Stairs
    I. Title   II. Blanc, Alan
    721.8′32

Library of Congress Cataloguing in Publication Data
A catalogue record for this book is
available from the Library of Congress

ISBN 0 7506 4846 5

Printed and bound in Great Britain

Contents

Foreword

It is cause for wonderment that the seemingly mundane device defined as 'a means of passing from one level to another by increments, more or less comforable – the vertical measures known as risers and the horizontal goings as treads' has, through history, generated such richly charged cultural and technical invention. The poetic extremes of human ingenuity are equally celebrated in the astonishing plastic virtuosity of Michelangelo's entry stair to the Laurentian library in Florence and the humbling simplicity of the early steps carved from a single log in Norway. Each symbolize deeply ingrained attitudes towards the world in a particular time and place, the means miraculously matching the ends.

At one moment the aspiration of stairs leading to heaven is frustrated in the tower of Babel, at the next they lead to sacrificial death in El Castillo, Chichén-Itzá in Mexico. Then again, Aalto demonstrated how a modest stair may generate the form of a small, secular masterpiece – grass steps lead to a raised court from which access to the entrance continues a progression, squeezing space, turning corners under filtered light first to deliver town councillors to their chamber and then, following the sequence, the public ascend three more steps to the gallery where their representatives may be observed in debate – this the Säynätsalo Town Hall in Finland which demonstrates democracy at work by means of a few judiciously disposed treads and risers!

Stairs serve as servant and master, as instrument and icon. The full range of symbolic and practical ends are obliged, however, to recognize the physical characteristics of the human body, each individual progression a miracle of balance and co-ordination requiring conscious effort and tactile contact as with no other element in our buildings.

The originator of this rewarding book, in his youth, sought safe refuge in the claustrophobic confines of the cupboard under domestic stairs during bombing raids on London, not, perhaps, the ideal conditions to generate inspiration. But it came. No doubt later, as contrast, he revelled in the vertiginous thrills of climbing to a virtual heaven through the structure of the Eiffel tower. The latter experience with its seductive imagery, celebrated in painting and photography, served as the epitome of what the twentieth century held in store – transparency, technology, the world viewed from above, humankind caught in a giant web. The stair through history as been solid, reassuring our passage. As traced in this book it has been transformed from its secure, compression-bound forebears to become a transparent, sometimes alarming, tensile instrument defying gravity, the excuse provided to display design virtuosity and liven private and public spaces and sculptural bravura.

Piranesi dreamt and drew stairs, but necessity bids us to transform such dreams into reality and a fine balance has been achieved, in this restructured, compressed and enhanced edition of *Stairs*, between the historical overview and everyday practicalities. The subsequent lifetime union of the small boy who emerged from under the stairs has been admirably consummated by his partner.

Allen Cunningham
London, 2001

1 Introduction

As I commenced the task of writing this book, I might have been asked 'Why another book on stairs?' This is, however, an abridged version of my husband Alan Blanc's book *Stairs, Steps and Ramps* which was published in 1996, the year after his death. True to Alan's thoroughness, the book was too long with too many illustrations and it was very expensive. I have now reduced it, in some cases by condensing the size of the diagrams, in others by omitting unnecessary examples, at the same time bringing in illustrations from recent buildings. The history of stairs has been omitted, but can be found on the publishers' website or, of course, in the original book.

Alan and I worked together for 50 years, first as students and then in architectural practice, and I was therefore very involved in the original book.

Alan had an obsession with stairs, starting with the London Blitz in 1940 when taking shelter night after night in the 'understairs' cupboard of his parents' Victorian terraced house. The actual space was of triangular section, panelled on one side, with a rough brick party wall on the other, whilst overhead there existed the full panoply of the carpenter's art, with glued and wedged treads and risers set into pine strings. The local ARP Warden advised 'understairs' for sheltering as the strongest structure within the home. A couple of houses further down the road were destroyed, so the young Blanc decided, as a game, to replan the family house in case theirs required

rebuilding. He measured up the structure, and found that the stair was the most difficult feature to plan. How long was each step and rise, and what about headroom – do you hit your head on the first floor landing? This was his earliest planning exercise into architecture and it is not surprising that architecture became his vocation five years later.

The second turning point followed with the sudden flush of funds that permitted a buying spree in Tiranti's around 1948. The purchases included two volumes of *L'Architecture Vivante, en Allemagne* (Erich Mendelsohn and Weissenhof) together with his most prized acquisition, Franz Schuster's *Treppen*. The book is pre-war but was resurrected and reprinted by Hoffman of Stuttgart in 1949. Schuster gave detailed advice with inspirational concern for geometry that makes the art of stair construction equal to furniture in terms of exactness and line (Figure 1.1). These volumes still sit on our bookshelf together with a number of other books on the same subject.

The greatest influence in Alan's architectural education was working for Walter Segal on leaving college, where the pros and cons of Franz Schuster were fully aired, Segal having known this work pre-war. Working with Walter meant drawing out staircases to full size, including the balustrade, pinning the tracing to the wall where the stair was to be installed in order that the visual effect could be fully established. These stairs were often very finely detailed, leaving

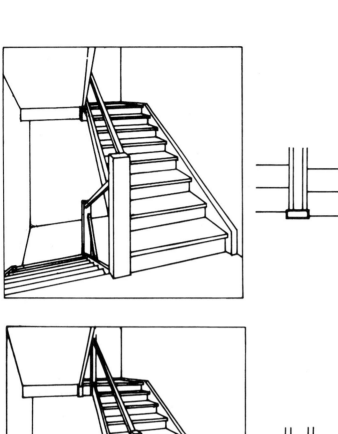

Figure 1.1 Variations at well end (from Schuster, F., Treppen, Hoffman Verlag, 1949)

a Solid newel at well end

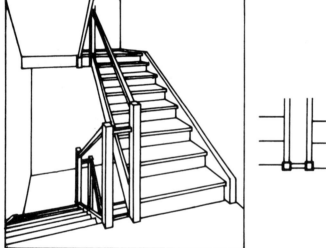

b Twin newels at well end

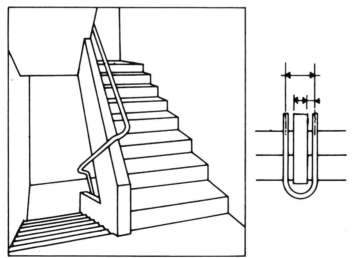

c Swept handrail (balustrade not shown but will infill between rail and strings)

almost an unsafe structure. Today, Codes of Practice and Section K of the National Building Regulations rule out those risks for domestic stairs where small children may use them unsupervised, but it is worth recalling that the minimal elegance achieved in the designs of Eva Jiricna is only obtainable by working in close collaboration with a qualified engineer, designing for public buildings where there are no children or where they are deemed to be supervised.

The historical references within *Treppen* started our interest in photographing stairs and in discovering the architecture of Gunnar Asplund, Roland Rohn or Otto Salvisberg that were drawn upon by Schuster. It is not possible to isolate the detailing solution from the context of the design. A typical example is Asplund's Courthouse at Gothenburg (Figure 2.7), where the movement sequence from entry court to loggia and stairhall leads with formal splendour to the courtrooms at first floor and thence by secondary means to the offices at upper levels. Such a 'promenade in space' is perhaps the finest achievement that well-designed stairs can attain. The open vertical circulation eloquently arranged at the core of buildings can certainly become the most captivating experience. Designs as diverse as Garnier's Paris Opera, Le Corbusier's Villa La Roche-Jeanneret and Lasdun's National Theatre in London all reveal the magic that is possible with creative designers.

Today, lifts and stairs as well as escalators form the core of all multi-storey plans, sadly often hidden behind solid enclosures to form uninteresting fire compartment zones. Modern technology using heat resistant glazing releases the architect from boxed-in solutions. Visual connection is once more feasible between vertical circulation and the spaces served. Pressure controlled environments can exclude smoke without recourse to the complication of double lobbies. Research for this book amongst older masterpieces in London often revealed that double lobbies are thwarted by having one set of doors permanently wedged open or simply propped ajar with a fire extinguisher. Today it is obligatory to provide access for the disabled, either by ramp or by stairlifts or hoists.

Outstanding developments such as the Lloyd's Building, London, or the Hong Kong and Shanghai Bank explore the new technologies and reveal that staircases and their modern equivalents can recapture the visual excitement that Piranesi (Figure 1.2) or Leonardo da Vinci awarded to stairs within the interior volume of their designs.

I hope that this new textbook will allow the reader to gain Alan's information in a condensed form, but at the same time to be enthused by our pictures and sketches. I hope Alan approves of my new version of his book.

Figure 1.2 An obsession with stairs, extract from Piranesi's Carceri, *Plate VII (from Scott, J., Piranesi, Academy Editions, 1975)*

2 Civic and public stairs

Steps and stairs have always been an essential part of building since primitive man first built a shelter. To be a few feet off the ground was to be protected against dangerous animals or the dampness of the ground in rainy periods. Ropes were twined from vegetation, or ladders formed from small branches tied together.

As time went by the various civilizations built their temples or place of worship to their gods. As the gods lived in the heavens such places were built high up on a mountain, or a high structure was erected if no mountain existed, and to get to the altar at the top a long ceremonial stair was created (Figures 2.1*a* and 2.1*b*). In Greek temples the floor or podium was raised approximately 1500 mm so that the crowd looked up at the priest in his aloof position. The Parthenon has a triple-block plinth, each block 500 mm × 750 mm, on the west front. Such a stylobate is difficult to scale and forms the intended barrier to the temple domain (Figure 2.1*c*). Roman temples were designed for the public to gain access to the altar spaces, thus a straight flight of stairs was created leading to the front entrance, as at Maison Carrée, Nîmes (Figure 2.1*d*).

Figure 2.1a A Jacob's ladder in landscape terms: steps called 'the skyladder' at Tai Shan, China (551 BC) (from Schuster, F., Treppen, *Hoffman Verlag, 1949)*

Figure 2.1b El Castillo, Chichén-Itzá, Yucatán, Mexico, thirteenth century (courtesy of Judith Blanc)

Figure 2.1c Parthenon steps

Figure 2.1d Direct flight at main entry to the Maison Carrée, Nîmes, 16 BC – the portico

2.1 Categories of stairs

The direct flight is the most popular ceremonial approach, but there are many ways of providing vertical circulation. Figure 2.2 depicts the various categories of stairs and shows the elaboration that can be achieved by adding turned steps or landings. Floor-to-floor heights are not always constant within buildings, and the strategy in adopting landings and return steps often helps to accommodate differing storeys without increasing the basic stairwell. The direct flight or single return version will occupy a greater floor area once the extent of upper landings is taken into account. The popularity of dog-leg or three-turn flights rests with the minimal core dimension required.

The three- and four-turn arrangements facilitate rotating the axis of approach. They also allow permutations to be made in terms of priority, landing by landing and turn by turn.

2.1.1 Direct flights

Direct flights of steps are often the most dramatic approach, particularly where they continue the line of movement from one level to the next on the main axis.

In the Renaissance the *palazzo* was frequently designed with the main state rooms on the first floor, the *piano nobile*. This was generally served by a grand, formal straight-flight stair. Key Renaissance examples are the grand staircase that

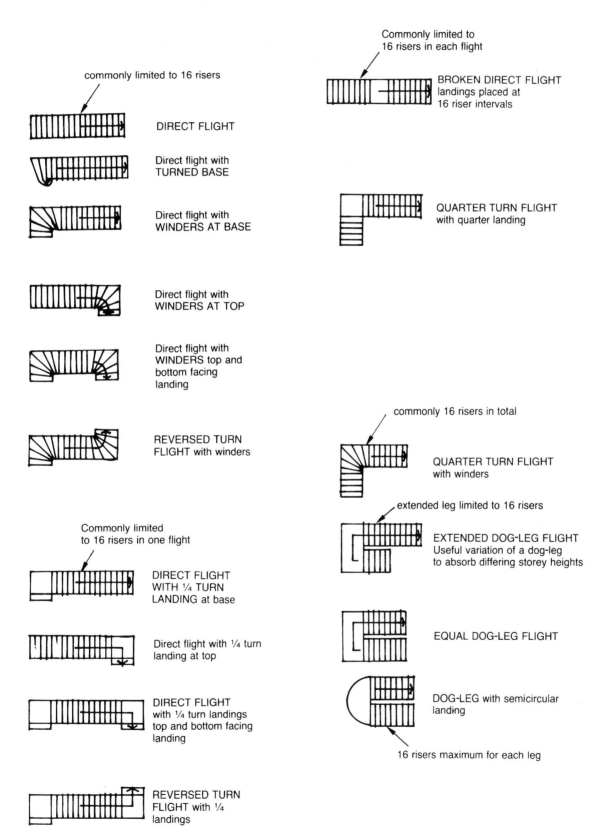

Figure 2.2 Key diagrams showing principal forms of steps

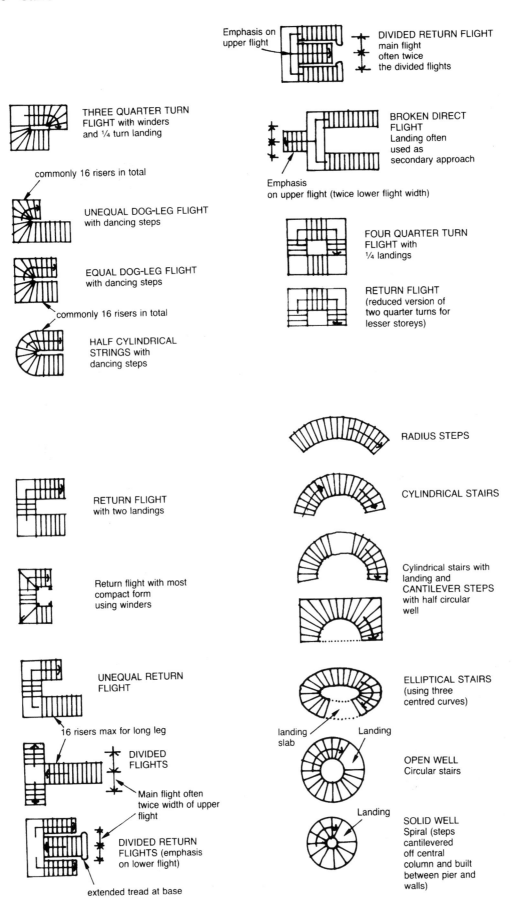

Figure 2.2 continued

leads to the Biblioteca Laurenziana, Florence, designed by Michelangelo in 1523–6 and completed by Giorgio Vasari in 1571 (Figures 2.3*a* and 2.3*b*), and the Palazzo Municipio, Genoa, 1564 (Figures 2.11*a* and 2.11*b*). Visitors were not expected to go up to the second floor so these stairs were utilitarian, hidden as a dog-leg, placed out of sight. In England, the same treatment was often used in stately homes, where the main entrance hall is the grand gathering place and the stair rises from there. A good example is Holkham Hall, Norfolk, 1734, executed by Matthew Brettingham (Figure 2.4).

One of the most impressive ceremonial stairs is at Hradcany Castle, Prague, 1920–2, by Jože Plečnik, where an impressive wide stair leads directly to the door of the main chamber (Figure 2.5).

Today there are many fine modern examples of the use of ceremonial stairs. At the Aarhus City Hall, 1937–42, by Arne Jacobson and Eric Møller (Figures 2.6*a–c*), the formal sequence follows a generous foyer placed below the Council Chamber, and the connecting formal steps are sited on the main axis with balconies leading to the first floor suite

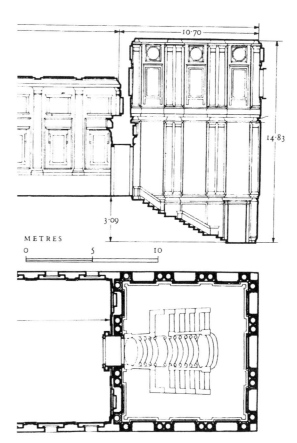

Figure 2.3b Biblioteca Laurenziana (from Ackerman, J. S., The Architecture of Michelangelo, *Penguin, 1970)*

(Figure 2.6*a*). A curving descending flight serves the cloakrooms and lavatories arranged out of sight in the basement (Figure 2.6*b*). The galleried atrium giving access to the general offices, which might unkindly be described as a modern-day penitentiary, is serviced by separate stairs and glazed lifts housed within a visible core at the end of the hallway. The contrast in finish and geometry between the richness of the entry and the simplicity of the office domain is sufficient to mark the different zones. The use of balcony and suspended forms to dominate the foyer makes a perfect foil to the spaces served.

Again, at the Courthouse extension at Gothenburg, by Asplund, 1937, the new

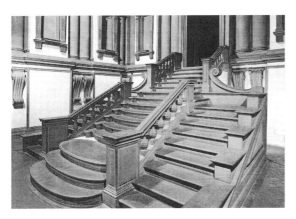

Figure 2.3a General view of Laurenzian staircase, constructed 1571 by Giorgio Vasari (courtesy of Kina Italia, Milano, Italy)

Figure 2.4 Holkham Hall, Norfolk

wing is placed at the edge of the older courtyard building (Figure 2.7*a–c*). The entry is turned through a right-angle, with the prospect of the new staircase rising behind a two-storey height window. The axis is turned again towards the cere-monial route to the first floor courts and to the glass enclosed lift. The principal rooms are laid out on three sides of the stairhall on both floors, and there is a separate stair at the end of the upper floor leading to offices for the court officials. The prece-

Figure 2.5 Ceremonial stairs, Hradcany Castle, 1920–2 (Jože Plečnik)

dence of the first floor is announced by the single monumental flight within a two-storey volume and signified by the greater ceiling height. The lighting levels to the staircase are also enhanced from the upper hall by clerestory lighting to balance the full-height glazing to the courtyard. The single flight appears to lightly bridge the 12 600 mm span although it is cleverly suspended by steel tubular sections from the floor beams overhead. The gentle proportion of tread to riser (360 mm to 110 mm) and the gracious sweep of the handrailing without breaks in alignment produce one of the most perfect stairs to look at and enjoy in use.

Ceremonial direct flights are frequently placed adjacent to a wall or situated between two walls. Oslo City Hall, which is almost contemporary, was largely built in wartime and signified an

emblem of resistance to Nazi occupation. The over-elaboration has to be seen as Norwegian self-expression in the face of adversity. The great inner hall has a Renaissance courtyard scale with a direct flight of gargantuan steps leading to the balconied upper floor designed for anti-clockwise movement through the public rooms (Figure 2.8).

In the Arthur Sackler Museum at Harvard, USA, 1984, Stirling and Wilford designed the staircase to be the spine ascending through the core of the plan. It has a central light well slotted into the length of the block with direct flights rising towards the light (Figure 2.9*a* and 2.9*b*). The lighting is gained via a fenestrated wall towards the office area. The tubular handrail is lit on the underside to give dramatic illumination at night. The same architects designed a similar stair at the Clore Gallery extension to the Tate in London (Figure 2.10), where the stairs to the principal space rise within a roof-lit well.

2.1.2 Multi-turn flights

The purpose of multi-turn design may well have been defensive. The approach stairs in citadels like the Alhambra are strategically planned for right-handed swordsmen fighting in defence. The attackers unless left-handed were under a disadvantage at every landing. The saving in space is another reason for multi-turn flights.

In the Renaissance such layouts arranged with upward approach enabled centrally placed stairs to be the main instrument in ordering plans with primary, secondary and minor circulations.

Double-return versions allowed the axis to be turned left or right, forwards or backwards. A prime example is the

Figure 2.6a Aarhus City Hall, 1937–42 (Arne Jacobsen and Eric Møller): Contrast in forms

Palazzo Municipio, Genoa, which has two prinicipal stairs. The first is used to separate the raised ground floor from the street. The second has the crucial role of turning the circulation back towards the important accommodation around the upper gallery (Figures 2.11*a* and 2.11*b*).

Figure 2.6c Aarhus City Hall: Glazed lifts

Figure 2.6b Aarhus City Hall: Curving stairs serving basement

Figure 2.7a Asplund's formal stairs at the Courthouse extension, Gothenburg, 1937

Figure 2.7b Detail of secondary stairs

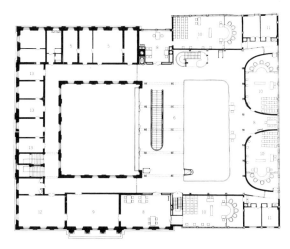

Figure 2.7c First floor plan

Figure 2.8 Oslo City Hall, 1937–50 (Anstein Arneberg and Magnus Poulsson). View of gargantuan steps within inner hall

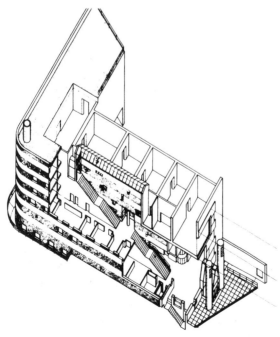

Figure 2.9a Arthur M. Sackler Gallery, Harvard, USA, 1984 (James Stirling, Michael Wilford and Associates). A diagram

Figure 2.9b Stair and light well

The Augustusburg at Brühl has a magnificent double-return stair as a centrepiece; the flights are in fact unequal to give a greater perspective to the upper ceiling. The *piano nobile* embraces the superbly scaled flights from both directions (Figures 2.12*a–d*). The open loggia at ground floor forms the carriage entrance with a sequence through the various courts, while the secondary openings lead to offices and service stairs. Neumann explored similar ideas in the entry hall at the Residenz in Würzburg, where the greater length of the 'return' flights enables the axis to be turned towards the central space (Figure 2.12*b*). It is a pattern used in many custom-made nine-

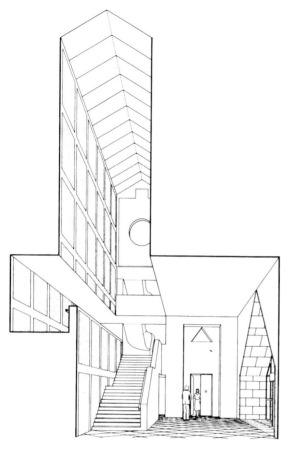

Figure 2.10 Entry to Clore Gallery, London, 1986 (James Stirling, Michael Wilford and Associates)

teenth-century art galleries, where the first floor gallery space requires a formal approach.

One of the most interesting derivations is the design made by Semper for the Kunsthistorisches Museum, Vienna (Figures 2.13*a–c*). This is archetypical of the central space stair applied to a large public building and certainly equal to palace planning of the Baroque era. The double courtyard arrangement has the main entry placed at right-angles through the centre wing; the spatial effect is enhanced by spatial volumes that penetrate to the upper storeys. The vestibule is domed with a mezzanine balcony to glimpse the first and second floors, arch-

ways open to the principal stairs which in turn lead the visitor to the rear of the entry hall. This ultimate landing is the starting point for a clockwise route through the impressive collection of Renaissance paintings. The mezzanine landing has return flights for the second floor rooms. There are screened service cores that link basement to roof level and that today contain passenger lifts for the disabled. The placement of volumes that open one to another within the centre wing is masterly and enables the building interior to be revealed in perfect order. One is never lost as to which direction to pursue.

A modern example of multi-turn stairs is the Royal Festival Hall, London, 1951, where the ground floor vestibule is an open space, with bars, cafés and exhibition spaces. The grand dog-leg stairs take visitors up on either side of the auditorium to the various galleries. The landings at each level overlook the fantastic window with views of the Thames and the riverside walk along the South Bank (Figures 2.14*a–d*).

2.1.3 Tapered flights

False perspective is a familiar device in landscape design but remarkable examples occur in interiors. Bernini's *scala regia* at the Vatican (Figures 2.15*a* and 2.15*b*) has to be seen as stage scenery to dramatize the passage of the Pope to the Sistine Chapel. The traditional ceremony involves a brief pause as the blessing is given from the top landing to the crowd assembled below. The tapered flight at Venturi's National Gallery (Figure 2.16) extension is in reverse, it has no claim to drama. It is, however, the principal public entrance for visitors to the main Italian art collection, starting in the entrance hall and

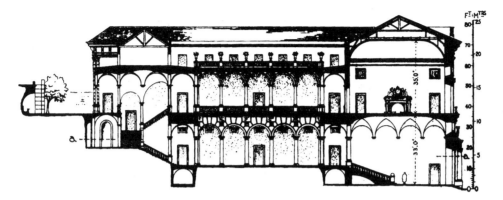

Figure 2.11a Palazzo Municipio, Genoa, 1564 (Lurago) (from Fletcher, B., A History of Architecture, *Batsford, 1954). A section*

widening up towards the main gallery, as opposed to the processional purposed by Bernini. His *scala regia* is in fact only used on formal occasions, apart from the low-ermost connection to St Peter's.

There are many good examples of external tapered stairs. One of the most successful is the work of Michelangelo at the Capitol, Rome (Figures 2.17*a* and 2.17*b*). The determining factors are the abrupt change of level between Via del Mare and the piazza and the further rise to the Palazzo Senatorio built over the ruins of the Tabularium. The primary route is via a long tapered ramp of steps

that terminates between a pair of giant statues of Dioscuri, made more dramatic by the reverse perspective. The arched fronts of the Conservatori and the Capitoline Museum are also canted in reverse alignment to enclose the full façade of the Palazzo. The final rise to the *piano nobile* is made externally with

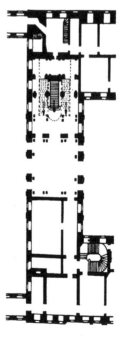

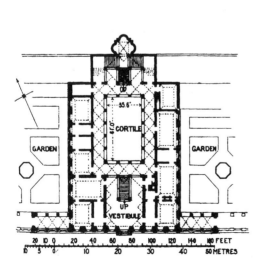

Figure 2.11b Plan

Figure 2.12a Baroque Palace Stairs, The Augustusburg, Brühl, Rheinland, 1743–8 (J. Balthasar Neumann). Outline plan of stairhall (from Schuster, F., Treppen, *Hoffman Verlag, 1949)*

Figure 2.12b Residenz, Wurzburg, Germany, 1723–43 (J. Balthasar Neumann). Use of return flight to turn axis back to central space

Figure 2.12d Rococo stairs, Schloss Brühl, 1748 (Neumann)

Figure 2.12c View of return flights within the central hall (courtesy of Steinhoff)

return stairs that link the piazza arcades to the entry portico at first floor. The real magic of the eccentric geometry is captured by the mounded star paving that connects the eye with each element – colonnade, fountain, ramp, stairs and the centrally placed equestrian statue of Marcus Aurelius. Functional requirements such as shelter and vehicles are met by a shaded serpentine path whilst today cars use a winding road tucked away to the side. The surfaces are picked out in contrasting materials, dark grey granite with white travertine blocks for risers and for the star pattern to the piazza.

2.2 Other types of stairs

2.2.1 The external approach

In some buildings the main approach is external with elaborate steps leading the

Figure 2.13a Kunsthistorisches Museum, Vienna, 1872–81 (Gottfried Semper): View from vestibule

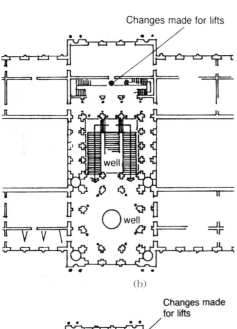

(b)

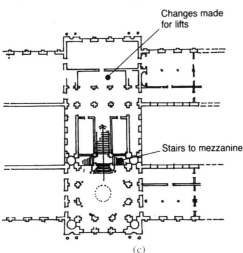

(c)

Figure 2.13b-c Kunsthistorisches Museum, Vienna: Outline plan, first floor; (c) Kunsthistorisches Museum, Vienna: Outline plan, ground floor

visitor to the front door on the *piano nobile*. Palladio often used this format, with turret stairs hidden within masonry piers. Chiswick House (Figure 2.18), a miniaturized copy of the Rotonda (Villa Capra), is a fine example, with elaborate steps on two façades leading to the main living areas. But the vertical circulation, both up and down, is situated in four turret stairs built into the masonry corners of the central octagonal saloon. The winders are very tight, being less than 1 000 mm wide. These minimal stairs show the social division of separate stairs for master and servant.

At the Hong Kong Shanghai Bank by Foster and Partners in 1986 (Figures 2.19 a–c), two escalators take customers from the open area on street level up to the banking hall at first floor. From there service cores with cloakrooms, subsidiary stairs and lifts, serve the upper offices, these cores forming features on the exterior.

2.2.2 Cylindrical and spiral stairs

Some of the most graceful forms of stair are the cylindrical and spiral. The primitive spiral is found in medieval castle towers where the stone steps rest one on top of another with the edges built into the surrounding walls.

Cylindrical stairs have been made as free-standing towers placed outside the building envelope. Some of the more ambitious designs permit horse and rider to ride up to the upper floors.

This is the explanation for the complex masonry construction at Blois (Figure 2.20) and which is built as a twin arcade to support the spiralling steps. It is said to have been influenced by Leonardo da Vinci.

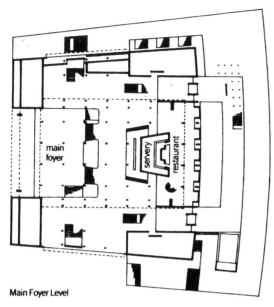

Main Foyer Level

Figure 2.14a Royal Festival Hall, London, 1951 (Sir Leslie Martin and Sir Robert Matthew): Key plan, foyer

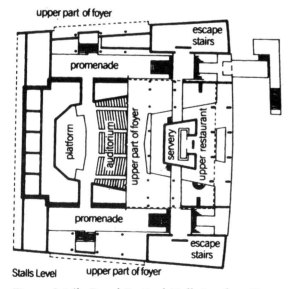

Stalls Level   upper part of foyer

Figure 2.14b Royal Festival Hall, London: Key plan, stalls

Figure 2.14c Royal Festival Hall, London: Stairs in relation to reception

Figure 2.14d Royal Festival Hall, London: Stairs in relation to foyer

A more ingenious solution inspired by the same artist connects the royal apartments at Chambord. The double circular stairs enable the royal path to be separate from the rest (Figures 2.21*a* and 2.21*b*), but at the same time the open nature of the balustrade allows the courtiers to admire royalty as they pass. The magnificent stonework forms the central feature of the cruciform plan and makes a complete contrast to the Palladian ideas of hiding away internal stairs. Another visual advantage at Chambord is the celebration of the cylindrical shape above the roof level where a domed lantern of Italian proportions towers over the giant chimney stacks. The practical purpose is to

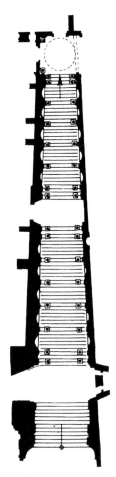

Figure 2.15b View of Scala Regia

Figure 2.15a Scala regia at the Vatican, 1661 (G. L. Bernini) (from Schuster, F., Treppen, *Hoffman Verlag, 1949). A plan*

light the double flight and the core of a plan that is over 42 m in depth. Doubling the flights is arranged with the simple expedient of stacking one above the other on 90° turns, the storey heights of 5700 mm permitting this solution. The da Vinci connection with Chambord is derived from the artist's sketches of four flights nesting one into the other.[1]

A modern example of a circular stair tower is Zublin-Haus (Gottfried Bohm) which is placed in a large glazed court (Figures 2.22*a* and 2.22*b*). The towers are linked to the office blocks on either side by bridges. This independent vertical

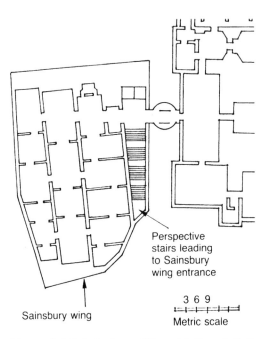

Perspective stairs leading to Sainsbury wing entrance

Sainsbury wing

3 6 9
Metric scale

Figure 2.16 Sainsbury Wing, National Gallery, London (Venturi)

Figure 2.17a The Capitol, Rome (Michelangelo): View of main flight to the Capitol

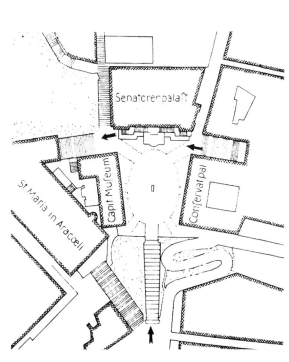

Figure 2.17b The Capitol Rome: Layout plan, first phase, 1540–1644, piazza paving (from Schuster, F., Treppen, *Hoffman Verlag, 1949)*

Figure 2.18 Turret stairs at Chiswick House, 1727–9 (Richard Boyle, 3rd Earl of Burlington) (from Summerson, J., Architecture in Britain 1530–1830, *Penguin, 1991, © Yale University Press)*

Figure 2.19a Hong Kong and Shanghai Bank, Hong Kong, 1986 (Foster and Partners): Escalators from street to podium

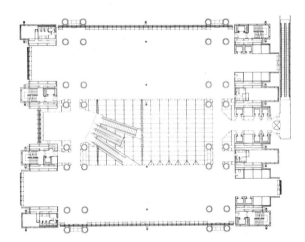

Figure 2.19b Hong Kong and Shanghai Bank, Hong Kong: Ground floor plan

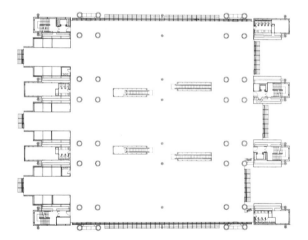

Figure 2.19c Hong Kong and Shanghai Bank, Hong Kong: Upper levels

circulation is preferred by Michael Hopkins in both Bracken House and the IBM Headquarters at Bedfont Lake.

The circular stair often forms the core of the plan. At the Nestlé HQ, Vevey, Switzerland (Jean Tschumi), where the graceful stair is placed on the axis of the 'Y' shaped complex (Figures 2.23*a–c*), it is placed within a generous circulation space. Like the double stair at Chambord, the stair has two flights one on top of the other. In this form it was not necessary to plan the floor landings to arrive at a specific axis point. In the basement stair at Aarhus, Jacobsen has solved this problem by designing the last

Figure 2.20 External staircase tower, Chateau de Blois, 1515–30

Figure 2.21a Double cylindrical stairs at Chambord, 1519–47

few steps as a straight flight. This can only be carried out if there is sufficient headroom (refer back to Figure 2.6b).

The helical theme has been used in two imaginative interiors. First in historical sequence, the exit ramp from the Vatican Museum, constructed in the 1930s (Figure 2.24), where the diameter of the stairwell reduces as one descends. The second is the more significant application at the Guggenheim Museum, New York, by Frank Lloyd Wright, 1956. This surely is an inspired development of the earlier idea and transforms the gallery spiral into the major element of the art gallery (Figures 2.25a and 2.25b). Purists

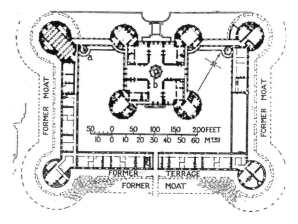

Figure 2.21b Key plan (from Fletcher, B., A History of Architecture, Batsford, 1945)

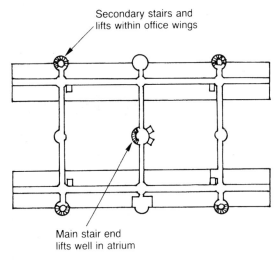

Secondary stairs and lifts within office wings

Main stair end lifts well in atrium

Figure 2.22a Zublin-Haus (Gottfried Bohm): Layout plan

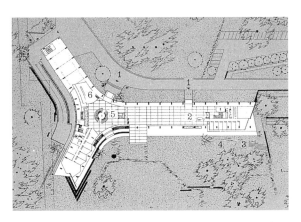

Figure 2.23a Nestlé HQ, Vevey (Jean Tschumi): Ground floor plan (from The New Nestlé International Headquarters in Vevey)

Figure 2.22b Zublin-Hans: Free-standing screen of lifts and stairs in central space

Figure 2.23b Nestlé HQ, Vevey: Elevation

Figure 2.23c Nestlé HQ, Vevey: Interior

Figure 2.24 Exit stairs, Vatican Museum

Figure 2.25a Gallery spiral, Guggenheim Museum, New York, 1956 (Frank Lloyd Wright): View downwards

Figure 2.25b Gallery spiral, Guggenheim Museum, New York: View upwards

will complain that paintings need horizontal alignment in the surrounding spaces to avoid conflicting views. Those critical aspects are not paramount when viewing pictures at the Guggenheim; the even lighting and the spacious layout give a balanced quality to the exhibition space, without the sloping lines of the floor becoming obstructive. It is true that the modest scale of wall area prevents very large exhibits being displayed. A more serious criticism is the low concrete balustrade. It does not prevent vertigo, although placed in a sloping plane and angled away from the ramp.

2.2.3 Theatrical stairs

A visit to the theatre is a time for exhibitionism. The theatrical use of stairs is more commonly associated with the vestibules to theatres and where vantage points of balconies and landings are visualized to show off the audience as they arrive and depart. The most celebrated promenade is that devised by Charles Garnier with the Grand Staircase at the Paris Opera (Figures 2.26a–c). It is worthwhile studying the plan in detail. The area employed almost equals the auditorium and is so arranged that the central well forms a theatre-sized space, overlooked by balconies

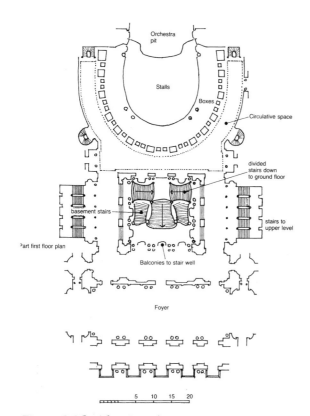

Figure 2.26a *The Grand Staircase, Paris Opera House, 1861–74 (Charles Garnier): Key plan at first floor*

Figure 2.26c *The Grand Staircase, Paris Opera House: Cut-away model of structure*

Figure 2.26b *The Grand Staircase, Paris Opera House: Half landing and balconies*

and foyers on all sides. The stairs rise to quarter landings with the upper flights forming bridges left and right. Wrought-iron framing enables the construction to run unsupported floor to floor. The ample proportions and space between solid and void allow the eye to take in the linear movement and for those climbing to the *piano nobile* to observe and to be observed, it is a truly magical space.

In the first scheme for the extension of the Royal Opera House by Jerome Dixon and Edward Jones, a grand stair was planned, but this was revised and now a long escalator takes the opera audience up to the auditorium without effort in the adjacent beautiful Floral Hall. An escalator is also used at the London Theatre where it travels upward when the theatre-

Figure 2.27 TV/AM offices and studios, Camden Town, London, 1983 (Terry Farrell). General view of landings and stairs

goers enter and downward when the play is over.

The stairhall and landings at TV/AM were conceived by Terry Farrell not simply as the central circulation space to the offices and studios but as a set piece for filming television (Figure 2.27). The movement left or right from the vestibule to the first floor is dramatized by landings or by groups of platform steps to gather people together. The variety of treatment permits variation in camera position whilst lighting effects can transform any location into a stage set.

Although not a stair for the theatre, the staircase at Les Galeries Lafayette, Paris (Figure 2.28) had a theatrical effect. This fantastic French Art Nouveau stair took shoppers from the ground floor trading area in this department store to the first floor. Although a structure of great signifi-

Figure 2.28 Sinuous stairs and balconies, Les Galeries Lafayette, Paris, early 1900s (stair designer, Louis Majorelle)

cance, it was demolished about 15 years ago in order to provide extra sales area on the ground floor. Obviously listing in France is not so vigorously upheld as in England. Escalators are now provided, tucked away from the main galleries.

Stairs for the movies are outside the usual building experience but the images hold the imagination. Architects such as Hans Dreir, Paul Nelson and Robert Mallet-Stevens, participated in many Hollywood masterpieces. The best remembered is probably the elliptical flight devised for the plantation home of Scarlet O'Hara in *Gone with the Wind*, designed by William Cameron Menzies. This full-scale mansion still stands on the back lot of Universal Studios, though remodelled for countless other epics. The other celluloid images today exist only on film. The greatest 'flights of imagination' were the special stages built for the Fred Astaire musicals and which had themes based upon multiple stairs (Figure 2.29).

2.3 Conclusion

A philosophic debate on whether stairs should have central or peripheral status cannot be concluded with a handful of examples. Further case studies are given at the end of the volume with the argument developed in differing directions.

Figure 2.29 Swing Time *(1936, George Stevens), United Artists, Director, Carrol Clarke*

There can be little doubt that the three-dimensional creativity that characterizes architecture from building is signified by the design skill displayed when handling staircases.

References

1 These sketches of quadruple stairs by Leonardo da Vinci are kept in the library of the Institute de France, MS B fol. 47.

3 Commercial stairs

3.1 Core planning and standardized stairs

Lift and stair cores in commercial buildings can be grouped according to building use – hotels, offices, retail and special facilities (such as multi-purpose layouts that contain conference and exhibition space). Building Codes in Britain stipulate minimal tread-to-rise relationships that vary according to the 'use' category;[1] these are dealt with in Chapter 10.

A wise designer ought to take the most generous proportion in multi-use buildings so that a common denominator in stair risers is maintained throughout. This means that standardized stairs can be made and a modular approach adopted to vertical dimensions within the total building section (Figure 3.1).

Under British Codes, the 180 mm riser × 280 mm tread provides the statutory minimum stair proportion for all categories of use within a multi-purpose design. Since 1999, however, there are new regulations on access for the disabled, and if a lift is not provided the stair has to be reduced to 170 mm maximum rise × 250 mm going. This ratio, however, does not match the comfort of the easy going 150 mm × 300 mm steps that served a similar role in the days of Sir Christopher Wren and which related to a brick module of 75 mm.

Today, commercial considerations play a dominant role in demoting stairs to a secondary place whilst lifts or escalators assume greater importance. Valuation surveyors run their rules over staircase dimensions to establish that minimal criteria have been applied since core plans do not count within the lettable area. The design process with hotels or offices must take this into account and every effort made to reduce wastage in core planning. In fact, larger scale layouts are worth developing at an early stage to establish options for floor-to-floor heights in relation to the size of stair shafts that have to be accommodated. A well 250 mm wide not only looks attractive but can absorb two risers at either end which in turn allows a 720 mm variation in storey height without increasing the overall size of the shaft (Figure 3.2). Floor areas and occupancy rates provide the traffic figures for lifts and stairs. Building Regulations allow a minimum of two steps, a single step being considered dangerous. Sizes for the former can be taken from installers' catalogues whilst the latter has to be approved by the fire brigade or licensing authority on means of escape in case of fire. The key dimensions relate to the maximum number of steps within an unbroken flight and the number and width of stairs needed for escape purposes.

Compactness with escape stairs can be achieved by stacking two sets of flights one above the other with a solid reinforced concrete wall separation (Figure 3.3a). A partial reinforced concrete fender wall, say 100–150 mm thick to infill the well, takes up less space than a

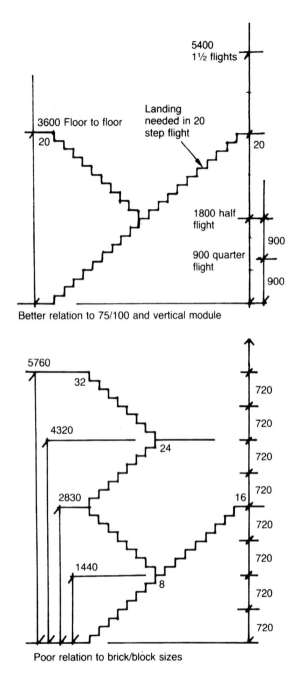

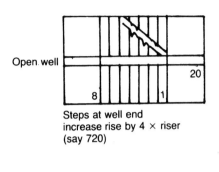

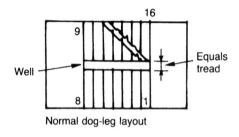

Figure 3.2 Steps at well end

Figure 3.1 Modular heights for steps

step in the length of the flight (Figure 3.3c). Chapter 8 details this construction.

The completion of the preparatory work can provide a matrix in establishing the repetitive upper floor plans whether hotel, office or retail. It is common practice to set out the main elements of the upper storeys in order to develop the 'footprint' of the buildings at ground level. The dichotomy that plagues core design rests with the attractions needed at entry level by comparison with the minimal qualities where immersed within lettable space at the upper floors.

The simplest solution is to unwind the principal flight into a more generous geometry at the entrance hall. A typical example is where a dog-leg design turns into an open well arrangement. Modern developments with fire resisting glazing can recapture transparency instead of stair shafts being hidden away in walled-off enclosures.

conventional metal balustrade, particularly with those designs that embrace swept handrailing at well ends (Figure 3.3b). A half-step relationship across the well in dog-leg stairs will ease the geometry of handrailing and only add half a

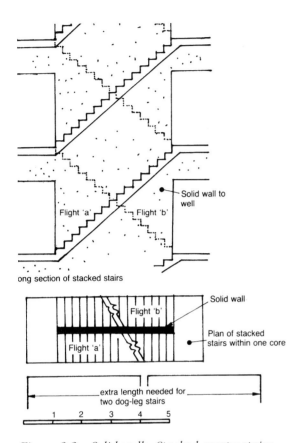

ong section of stacked stairs

Flight 'a' Flight 'b'

Solid wall to well

Solid wall

Flight 'b'

Flight 'a'

Plan of stacked stairs within one core

extra length needed for two dog-leg stairs

1 2 3 4 5

Figure 3.3a Solid wells: Stacked escape stairs

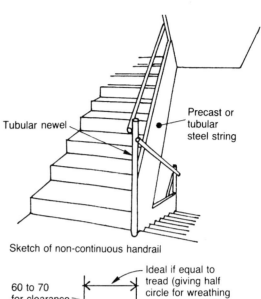

Tubular newel

Precast or tubular steel string

Sketch of non-continuous handrail

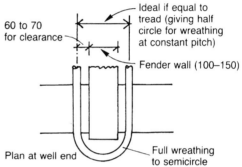

60 to 70 for clearance

Ideal if equal to tread (giving half circle for wreathing at constant pitch)

Fender wall (100–150)

Plan at well end

Full wreathing to semicircle

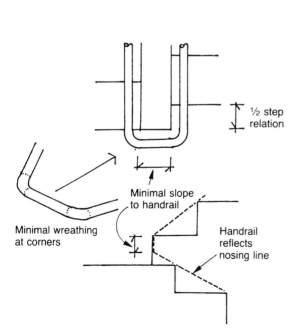

½ step relation

Minimal slope to handrail

Minimal wreathing at corners

Handrail reflects nosing line

Figure 3.3c Solid wells: Half-step relationship

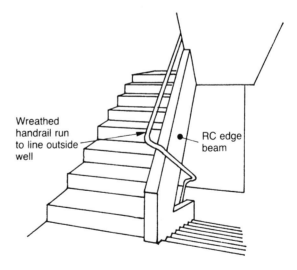

Wreathed handrail run to line outside well

RC edge beam

Figure 3.3b Solid wells: Fender walls

3.1.1 Office core locations

The salient dimensions relate to the maximum escape run from the furthest corner of the working area to the safety of the enclosed stairs. Protected lobbies or passages can extend these lengths. The basic arrangement is given in Figures 3.4a–c with guidance on limiting factors in the UK and abroad.

The core locations depend upon the floor configuration adopted. For high rise, slab block versus tower has to be considered. For medium rise, further comparisons need to be made with atrium and courtyard forms as well as geometries involving irregular-shaped buildings. Figures 3.5 and 3.6 provide a diagrammatic guide with references to typical designs. The obvious criteria from the economic viewpoint are core sizes that can be expressed as the smallest proportion of the rental and usable floors. For users there is another critical factor, namely the largest areas that can be accommodated at any single floor despite breaks incurred through lift and stair locations. The present interest with atria-based forms has produced deep floor plans of extended 'racetrack' layout with cores distributed along the edges, as at No. 1 Finsbury Avenue (Figures 3.7a–c). Triple-bay depths have the advantage of layering plans so that the central zone can accommodate cores and servant spaces with the daylit outer zone used for prime activity. Racetrack plans of these patterns are used for highly serviced office buildings. They also apply to educational facilities, hospitals and laboratories where servicing is centrally located.

More extreme separation in the elements can be seen at the Lloyd's Building, London, and with the Hong Kong and Shanghai Bank where external towers provide lift and stair cores. These 'servant' features are placed outside the uninterrupted volume of atria and related offices. The escalators for both buildings are illustrated in detail in Figures 2.19 and 11.5).

3.1.2 New directions

The reconstruction of the former Financial Times building (Bracken House) by Michael Hopkins and Partners has achieved a unique subdivision, with the central atrium and lift cores placed at the maximum permitted remove from the compartmented escape stairs and remodelled areas within the retained wings of the former layout (Figures 3.8a and 3.8b). Accommodation stairs are sited on either side of the new open offices and permit direct connection between the floors throughout the eight storeys. The perforation of compartment floors is allowed owing to the sprinkler system installed throughout the common office accommodation and to the fact that four new escape stairs are strategically designed at either end of the retained wings. A further benefit of the layout with outward escape from the atrium lift lobby is relaxation of fire enclosure to the main vertical circulation. The steelwork is uncased and the fenestration openable between working areas and atrium and hallways. It is another version of the Bradbury Building in Los Angeles (Figure 3.23) but more compact and relevant to today's working needs. The role played by the vertical circulation elements recognizes the changed importance, with lifts having primary importance and featured within the atrium as wall climbers, with the structural support given by steel plate towers (Figure 3.8c). The circular

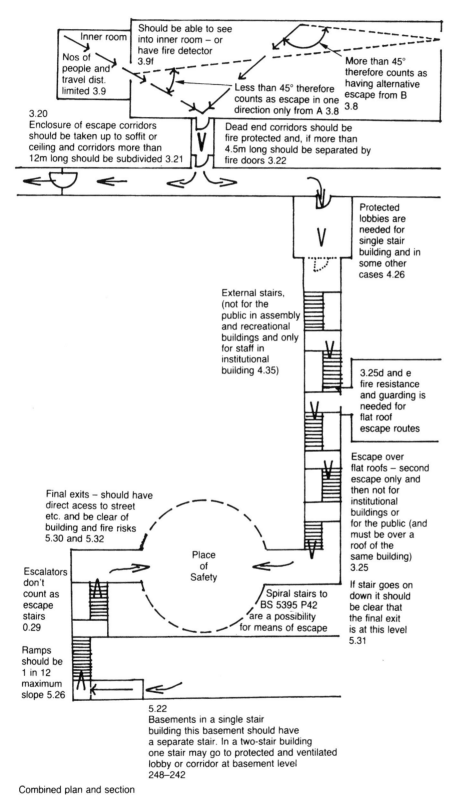

Inner room

Should be able to see into inner room – or have fire detector 3.9f

Nos of people and travel dist. limited 3.9

More than 45° therefore counts as having alternative escape from B 3.8

Less than 45° therefore counts as escape in one direction only from A 3.8

3.20
Enclosure of escape corridors should be taken up to soffit or ceiling and corridors more than 12m long should be subdivided 3.21

Dead end corridors should be fire protected and, if more than 4.5m long should be separated by fire doors 3.22

Protected lobbies are needed for single stair building and in some other cases 4.26

External stairs, (not for the public in assembly and recreational buildings and only for staff in institutional building 4.35)

3.25d and e fire resistance and guarding is needed for flat roof escape routes

Escape over flat roofs – second escape only and then not for institutional buildings or for the public (and must be over a roof of the same building) 3.25

Final exits – should have direct acess to street etc. and be clear of building and fire risks 5.30 and 5.32

Place of Safety

Escalators don't count as escape stairs 0.29

Spiral stairs to BS 5395 P42 are a possibility for means of escape

If stair goes on down it should be clear that the final exit is at this level 5.31

Ramps should be 1 in 12 maximum slope 5.26

5.22
Basements in a single stair building this basement should have a separate stair. In a two-stair building one stair may go to protected and ventilated lobby or corridor at basement level 248–242

Combined plan and section

Figure 3.4a Core limitations for commercial buildings: Limitations imposed by National Building Regulations

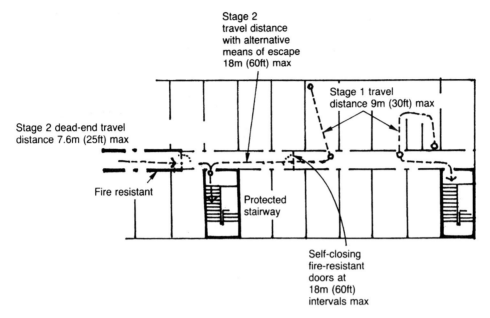

Figure 3.4b Typical specified travel distances to stairways in a hotel building given by international planning guides

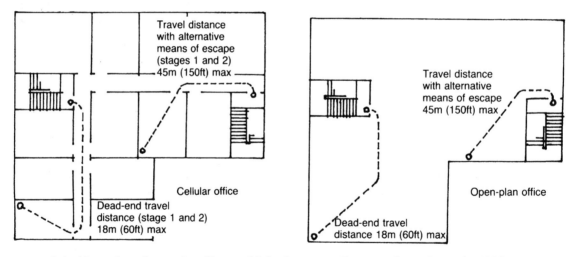

Figure 3.4c Typical guidance for offices published in West Germany from the early 1980s

accommodation stairs are the next most-used element, whilst the wings contain the four new escape routes and ancillary lifts. In case of fire, the fire brigade teams would tackle the problem from the wings where allocated lifts and dry risers are sited either side of the open plan area. The layout combining new and old elements on the Financial Times site has pro-

duced a new concept of conservation and one that shows the most interesting combination of technology in arranging lifts and stairs today.

The other reconstruction indicating changes in attitude to fire safety is the story of the Economist Building in relation to the original core plan (circa 1964) and the remodelling undertaken in 1992.

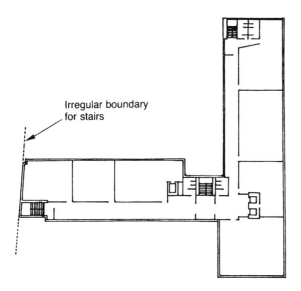

Figure 3.5a Core arrangements for offices: Single zone layout: main stair and lifts at junction of two wings, with secondary stairs at ends of corridors

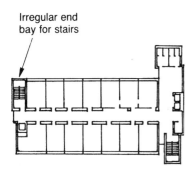

Figure 3.5b Double zone layout: spine corridor form with main stair, lifts and service area to one end and secondary stair and lift at opposite end

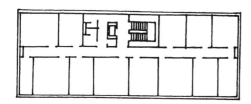

Figure 3.5c Double zone layout with central core: typical single staircase design for low-rise could however form a pattern for development with equal sized cores spaced at intervals in length of block

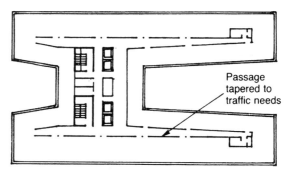

Figure 3.5d Double zone layout using H or U form, typical pattern to devise window walls to all sides of offices. Variations include V, X and Y forms around core zones

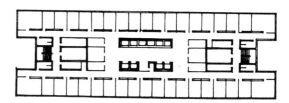

Figure 3.6a Multiple bay plans: Triple zone layout with parallel corridors and central core (Phönix-Rheinrohr AG Germany Competition 1955)

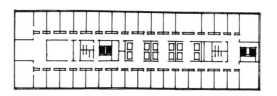

Figure 3.6b Triple zone with racetrack plan enclosing central core (Phönix-Rheinrohr AG Germany Competition 1955)

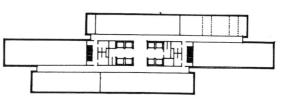

Figure 3.6c Staggered triple zone layout (Phönix-Rheinrohr AG Germany 1957, scheme completed). Architects: Helmut Hentrich and Hubert Petschnigg

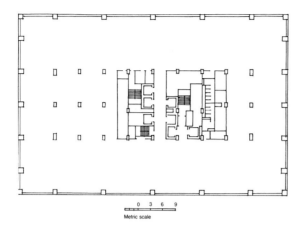

0 3 6 9
Metric scale

Figure 3.6d Multiple bay plans: Open layout for high rise tower, John Hancock Center, Chicago, Illinois, 1969, Architects: SOM

The building, like Bracken House, falls under the Section 20 legislation that applies to 'over cube' premises in Inner London; for definition refer to Chapter 10.

The initial designs had to comply with the former requirements of the London Fire Brigade to have facilities to climb directly onto escape stairs in case of lift failure. Such demands, with internally sites stairs, meant two open-air shafts within the core. Each shaft had a rung ladder accessible to windows on both escape route landings (Figure 3.9a). It was a solution favoured in old Parisian apartment blocks. The changes brought about by 'positive' air pressure devices for stair and lobbies have revolutionized the layout of inner cores. At the Economist Building it enabled service areas to be enlarged to contain a kitchen as well as male and female lavatories at every floor as opposed to alternate levels (Figure 3.9b).

3.1.3 Hotel core details

Lift and stair locations in hotels depend upon permitted lengths of protected corri-dors serving bedroom accommodation[2] and have to relate to the building's footprint at entry level. This is not necessarily related to the street but to the upper part of the podium, as many hotels rise above one or more floors of commercial shopping. The Renaissance Center, Detroit (Figure 3.10a), is a good primer. Here, escalators, lifts and escape stairs serve the podium with a transfer to the main core within the entry to the hotel, to afford greater security.

Many Portman-designed hotels[3] dramatize the entry zone with a vast atrium surrounded by galleries served by wall-climber lifts top to bottom of the space (Figures 3.10a and 3.10b). A modest variation is the Hilton Hotel, London Airport, where the lifts form a vertical feature within a generous atrium. The bedroom wings are entered by open galleried bridges on either side of the lift shaft, whilst the fire stairs are lost within the bedroom wings to accord with British Regulations (Figures 3.11a and 3.11b).

The final examples demonstrate the key roles of staircases in older buildings. Firstly, there is the Ritz Hotel, London, designed by Mewès and Davis in the early 1900s. The 'U' shaped plan placed the main façade to Piccadilly with return wings to Green Park. The sequence of public spaces runs east to west, with a large open-well stair placed as an eye-catcher turned towards the principal suites at first floor (Figure 3.12). Lift lobbies and secondary stairs occur off the main axis but are subservient to the grand stairs first glimpsed off the main entry.

By contrast, the Lanesborough Hotel is a conversion from the former St George's Hospital of 1827. The new internal circulation has been resited to emphasize lifts and vestibules while the former stairhall now

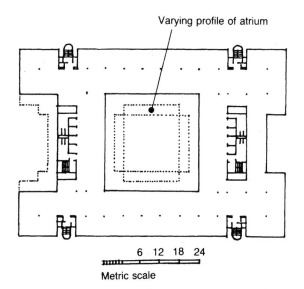

Figure 3.7a No. 1 Finsbury Avenue: Deep plan zones around atria spaces. The dimensions permit roughly consistent depth of office from fenestration

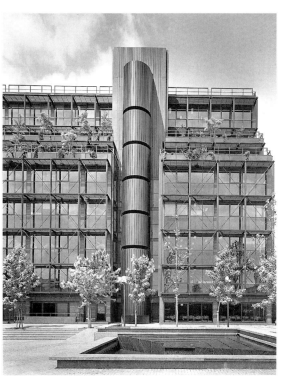

Figure 3.7c No. 1 Finsbury Avenue, City of London, 1985, Architects: Arup Associates: Façade with stair nodes expressed as towers

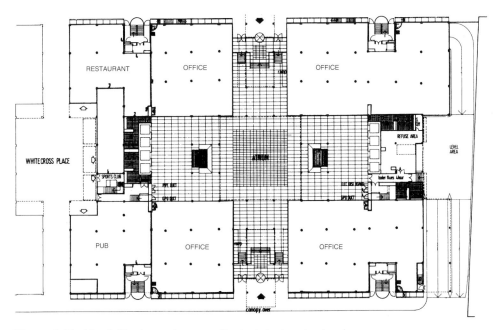

Figure 3.7b No. 1 Finsbury Avenue: Footprint at entry level

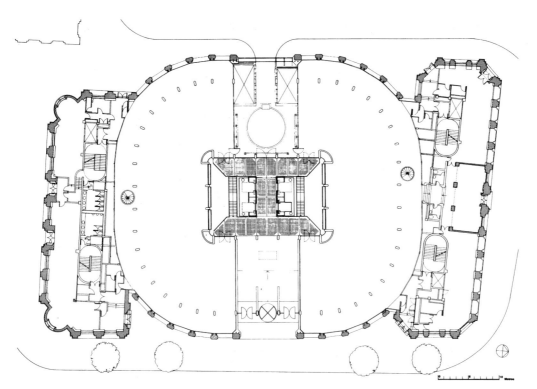

Figure 3.8a Bracken House, City of London, 1992, Architects: Michael Hopkins and Partners: Plan at street level

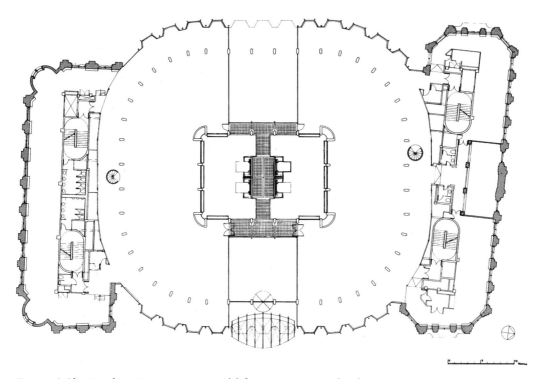

Figure 3.8b Bracken House: Atria and lift cores at upper level

Figure 3.8c *Bracken House: Steel plate towers to support wall-climber lifts (courtesy Alan Delaney, Wordsearch)*

has a minor function and relates simply to the basement dining area. The scale of the remodelled hallway is a reminder of the grandeur of stairs before lifts took over in hotel planning (Figure 3.13).

3.1.4 Escalators, lifts and stairs in major spaces for retail and related buildings

The nineteenth-century department store and the great exhibition halls of that period are the twin sources for a whole range of building types. The main stair provided the great exhibition space around which the display area was designed. Perhaps the greatest of these was Les Galeries Lafayette, Paris, in the 1900s (Figure 2.28), but fashion and commercialism took away the stairs leaving only the galleries with their Art Nouveau balustrading

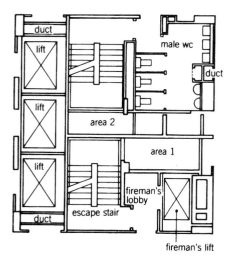

Figure 3.9a *The Economist Building: Original Core, 1964, Architects: Alison and Peter Smithson in association with Maurice Bebb*

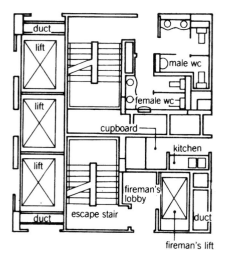

Figure 3.9b *The Economist Building: Reconstructed core, 1990, Architects: SOM*

designed by Louis Majorelle. The work by Hector Guimard in the same style has been better preserved at many of the entrance stairs to the Paris Metro (Figure 3.14).

Similarly, the lifts at Selfridges, London, were very elaborate and formed a great feature of the store (Figure 11.5*e*) but now, although lifts still exist with modern lift doors, three new banks of escalators provide customers with easy vertical movement through the five floors. The

Figure 3.10a Portman-designed hotels: Renaissance Center, Detroit, 1977. General view of multi-storey mall below hotel towers

Figure 3.10b Portman-designed hotels: Hyatt Regency, Detroit, 1970s. Wall-climber lifts playing a dramatic role within heavily shaped structure

logic is that if customers can see the various merchandise as they move up or down they may be tempted to get off and purchase. This is not possible within an enclosed lift.

The galleried stairhall or atrium of the Electricity Board, Prague, was completed in 1935, designed by Adolf Bens and Josef Kriz (Figure 3.15). The construction is reinforced concrete with a top-lit roof formed by glass blocks set in concrete ribs. The triple return flight is lit dramatically from the landing windows and forms a complete composition to the end wall. Lift clusters are placed in lobbies left and right of the main hall.

In Britain the first taste of pre-war modernism in store interiors can be seen with the freely arranged floors and sweeping escalators within the John Lewis Store, Oxford Street, of 1939.[4]

Today's store or shopping mall deploys escalators, lifts and stairs as 'accommodation' routes to the key levels within the cavernous interiors. Ideally the public should be able to explore the sequence of spaces in a logical manner (Figures 3.16a and 3.16b). The illustrations reveal the enticing way escalators or linkways are placed as nodes within a shopping mall to attract movement between floors. A logical flow both inwards and outwards from stores will be endorsed by the fire brigade but thought to be less important by many shopkeepers. Their brief 'to entice the public in' is often more important than finding a convenient circulation back to the shop entrance. An exemplary case for clarity of movement via escalators

Figure 3.11a Central Lifts, Hilton Hotel, London Airport, 1990, Architects: Michael Manser Associates (courtesy of Michael Bryant)

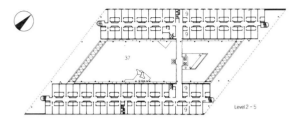

Figure 3.11b Central Lifts, Hilton Hotel, London: Key plan

is the John Lewis Store in Kingston-upon-Thames. The naturally lit space is bridged by an elegant array of moving stairs from floor to floor. Graphics exist hardly at all as they are not needed within the sales areas other than to locate fire escapes (Figure 3.17). The success of the store has meant that extra escalators have

Figure 3.12 Grand staircase, Ritz Hotel, London, 1905, Architects: Mews and Davis

Figure 3.13 Remodelled stairs and hall, The Lanesborough Hotel, Hyde Park Corner, 1992, London, Architects: Fitzroy Robinson (slide from the hotel)

Figure 3.14 Forms emulating lily leaves and tendrils, entry to the Metro, Paris, 1900, Architect: Hector Guimard

Figure 3.16a Covered malls: Shopping mall, Malmo, 1960s (designer unknown)

Figure 3.15 Pre-eminence of stairs, Electricity Board offices and showrooms, Prague, 1935, Architects: Adolf Bens and Josef Kriz

Figure 3.16b Covered malls: Node locations with well-placed stairs and linkways, Georgetown Mall, Washington, DC, 1980s (designer unknown)

Figure 3.17 Interior of John Lewis Store, Kingston-upon-Thames, 1990, Architects: Ahrends Burton and Koralek (courtesy of Chris Gascoigne)

been added parallel to the existing to improve circulation.

The use of mechanical means of movement has transformed retailing design into a vertical pattern of developments, with banks of lifts and stairs set out as the key viewing point for the store interior. The concept has been transferred to multiple use buildings that might embrace hotels, offices and shops within a vertical atrium. Water Tower Place, Chicago, has the drama of escalators rising directly from the street plus glazed lifts that serve the multi-storey mall. The elevated moving stairs and exciting lifts create a new art

form (Figures 3.18*a* and 3.18*b*). The success rests upon the innate curiosity of people to ascend and move to brighter elements in the interior. Vertigo is combated by tinted glass balustrades, ledges and high-level handrailing.

3.2 Accommodation stairs

Accommodation stairs are defined as additional or amenity stairs in excess of means of escape provisions. In reality accommodation routes often form the most conspicuous features within com-

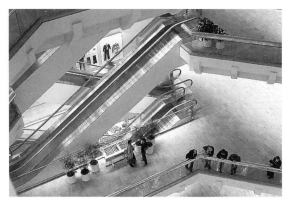

Figure 3.18a New art form for escalators and lifts: Water Tower Place, Chicago, 1976, Architects: Loebl, Schlossman, Bennett and Dart

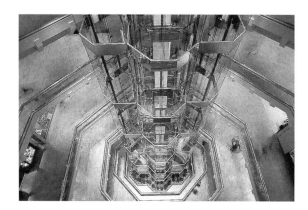

Figure 3.18b Another view of Water Tower Place

mercial interiors. The key role is to link the crucial zones of the building, not only by moving people but with the creation of a visual interconnection between the storeys. Portman's hotel designs are obvious examples where escalators, lifts and stairs are all employed to full theatrical effect within a vast atrium.

The benefits occur with more modest schemes, particularly in two- and three-storey buildings where a stairwell allows the interior to be open to view. Eva Jiricna's well-known designs[5] often relate to stores where movement through the various spaces is celebrated by the most imaginative flights of steps. The Joseph Store in Sloan Street is the best known example (Figures 3.19*a* and 3.19*b*). The use of glass and open framing gives the

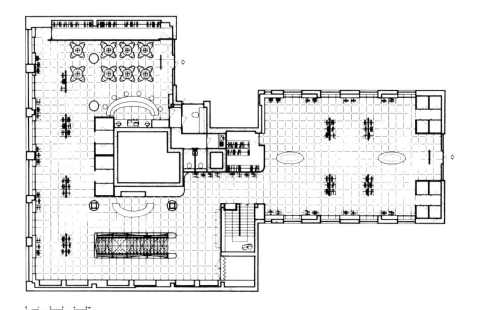

Figure 3.19a Accommodation stairs by Eva Jiricna: Layout plan, Joseph Store, Sloane Street, London (see Figures 7.7a–c for details)

Figure 3.19b Interior space, Joseph Store

least interruption to the eye. Curving forms can be used to advantage to form an open cylinder within the plan. An imaginative play on this theme occurs within the Gerschaftshaus, Vienna, designed by Hans Hollein. Here, the ascending geometry is created to afford views to each corner of the complex (Figure 3.20). The circular land-

ings or stairs in differing widths are placed in differing planes to improve the upward perspective, encased lifts are placed alongside for functional servicing floor by floor, while the centrepiece is a veritable 'house of stairs' providing as much enjoyment as the Stiegenhaus in Brühl.

The adjustment of stair widths is a feature used in nineteenth-century hotels whereby the width reduces with ascent, this providing a tapering well and increasing the spacious quality when looking up the central well. This idea works well with three-turn designs within a squarish geometry (Figure 3.21).

Two examples from the late nineteenth century are worth noting as new building types were developed. One is the Hallidie Building, San Francisco (Figure 3.22), where the architect devised the escape stairs as the principal feature, placed externally to the fully glazed façade. The other, the most inspirational of atrium interiors, was the open metal stairs and visible lift shafts used by George H. Wyman in the Bradbury Building, Los Angeles (Figure 3.23).

Figure 3.20 Curving forms, Gerschaftshaus, Vienna, 1990, Architect: Hans Hollein

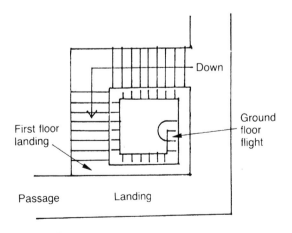

Figure 3.21 Increasing well size

Figure 3.22 Hallidie Building, San Francisco, 1917, Architect: Willis Polk

Figure 3.23 Bradbury Building, Los Angeles, 1893, Architect: George M. Wyman

References

1 Refer to a useful guide entitled *The Building Regulations* by Powell Smith and Billington (11th edn), 1999, published by Blackwell Science. Note that different regulations apply to Scotland.
2 Most major hotel groups produce design guides concerned with space standards, the sections related to protected cores and stairs being of greatest value.
3 Portman's remarkable oeuvre is best seen in a book entitled *The Architect as Developer* by Portman and Barnett, 1976.
4 The John Lewis Partnership employed Slater and Moberly as project architects for both the Oxford Street Store (1938–9) and for the Mendelsohnian Peter Jones Store, Sloane Square (1935–7). The latter design, however, had the inspired benefit of a gifted designer William Crabtree as well as Professor Charles Reilly as consultant.
5 For Eva Jiricna designs refer to *Eva Jiricna Designs in Exile* by Martin Pawley, 1990, published by Fourth Estate & Wordsearch.

4 Domestic stairs

4.1 Generic plans

The layout of both houses and flats can be summarized on a generic basis,[1] i.e. the allocation of minor and major zones for service spaces and habitable areas respectively. Broadly speaking, the minor zones are associated with stairs, bathrooms, kitchens, utility areas as well as small single bedrooms or studies, while major zones are made up of the living rooms and the larger bedrooms. If the assumption is made that all rooms shall be accessible from the common stairhall to avoid using habitable areas as passageways, plan variations are effectively limited for the smaller house to two basic forms. First is the 'Universal' plan (Figures 4.1a and 4.1b) and its modification for long-fronted formation (Figures 4.1c and 4.1d). With narrow-fronted, semi-detached or terraced houses the stair can be placed across the house, allowing for a front living room of 4500 mm. The artisan house of the turn of the century often had an entry door off the side passage between two houses. A shared access 900 mm wide, allowing for the party and external walls, gives a site width of

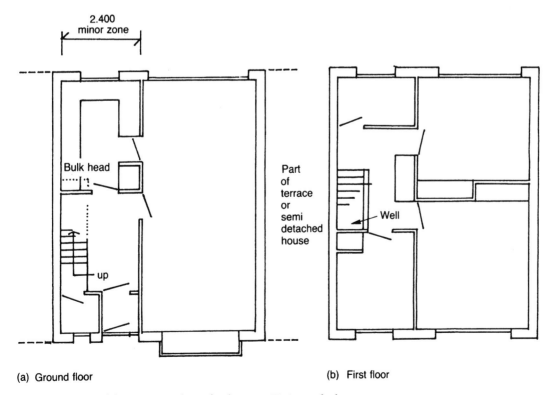

(a) Ground floor

(b) First floor

Figure 4.1a and b Generic plans for houses: Universal plan

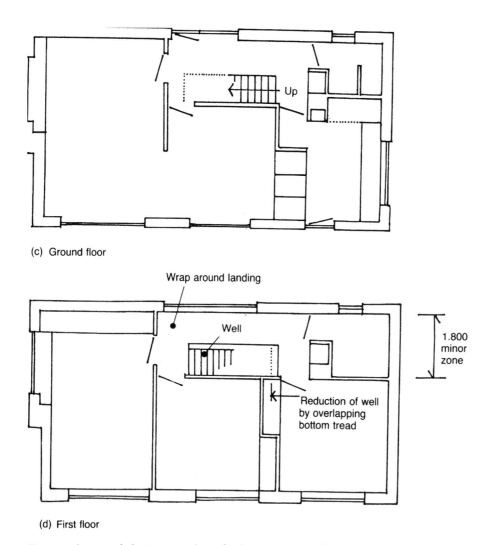

(c) Ground floor

(d) First floor

Figures 4.1c and d Generic plans for houses: Turned universal plan

5 325 mm. If the entrance is on the front with terraced houses, the front room will be reduced to 3 500 mm (Figure 4.1*e*).

Second, for wider frontages, is the 'Double Fronted' plan and its wealth of central core layouts (Figures 4.2*a–g*). The Building Regulations are set out in Chapter 10. The minimum width of stair allowed is 800 mm, but if planned between walls a dimension of 900 mm is necessary to enable furniture to be negotiated to the first floor. A hallway of a similar dimension is also required and, allowing for a well and balustrade,

a core dimension of 1 800 mm is needed.

Standard stairs are available off the peg which give a floor-to-floor height of 2 600 mm: 12 treads of 216 mm and overall going of 2 700 mm.

4.2 Staircase options

4.2.1 Direct flights

The single direct flight provides the cheapest constructional solution. If laid

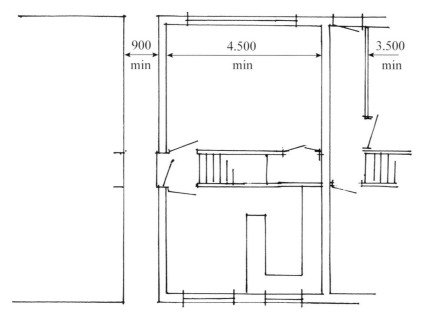

Figures 4.1e Generic plans for houses: Side entry house

out across the plan it will give the most compact answer (Figure 4.2*a*). This minimal aspect explains its use in cottage architecture where there are no halls or lobbies. In the simplest plans, the staircase would rise directly opposite the street door with the accommodation arranged to one or both sides. In these cases, living areas or bedrooms were used as 'through rooms' to keep the envelope walls to the absolute minimum, often as small as 30 square metres per floor (Figure 4.2*b*).

In a wide-fronted plan the same direct flight set longitudinally incurs a 'wrap around' hall at each floor level. A slight saving on this extravagance can be achieved when the well is returned at first floor over the second riser, providing the required headroom of 2 000 mm is available (Figure 4.1*d*). A solution by Walter Segal (Figures 4.2*d* and 4.2*e*) gives an oriel landing, which shortens the hall by 450 mm and also provides a sheltering porch at the entry. The single top step does not comply with current

National Building Regulations in the UK. Two steps do, and should give the necessary headroom. In times past non-conforming use with the meanest winders, coupled with 200 mm × 200 mm treads and risers, enabled Dutch designs to reach the ultimate levels of parsimony. The stairs in old Amsterdam houses have ladder-like steps more appropriate to ships than residences. This is the reason why old Dutch houses sprouted gable pulley blocks so that beds, chests and wardrobes could be hauled up externally and passed through upper windows. Scotland's 'turret' houses had the restriction of helical or multi-turn flights with a central pier. The problem was solved by making the large furniture on site, room by room, and leaving it there for posterity!

Winders to the mandatory taper are permitted and will reduce hallways by 900 mm, but it is better to keep these at the base of the stair for safety. It is worth remembering that a quarter turn of winders equals four treads and that the

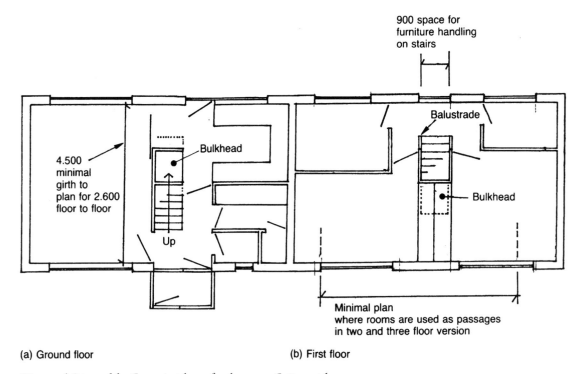

(a) Ground floor   (b) First floor

Figure 4.2a and b Generic plans for houses: Cottage plan

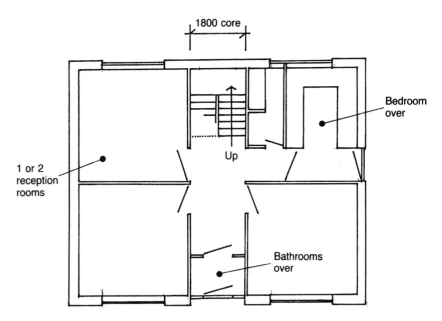

Figure 4.2c Generic plans for houses: Double-fronted Georgian plan

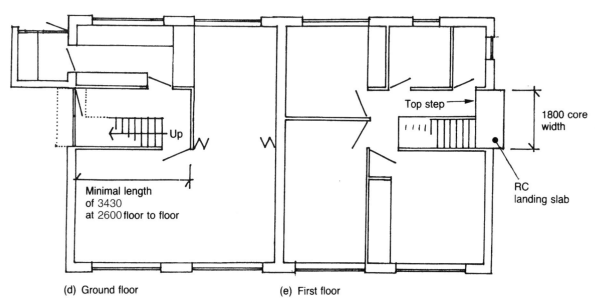

Figures 4.2d and e Generic plans for houses: Turned double-fronted plan

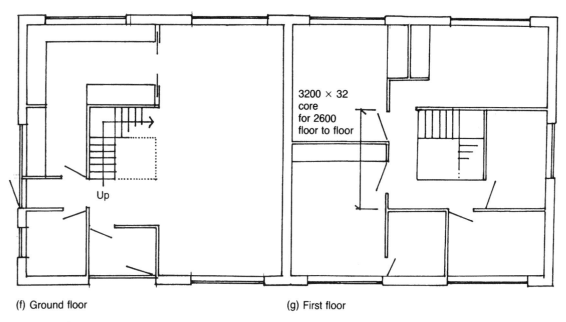

Figure 4.2f and g Generic plans for houses: Central core plan

arrangement can successfully reorder a hallway to give more space for furniture (Figure 4.3*b*). For variations with winders refer back to the details in Chapter 2 (Figure 2.2). Purists will say that it should be possible to design without tapered or winding treads; pleasure put forward in relation to comfort and safety in use, particularly for the less physically able. The straight flight and a full-length handrail are much preferred by them to coping with awkward treads, which are too far from

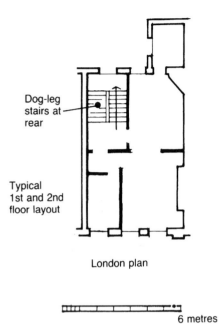

London plan

6 metres

Figure 4.3a London plan (based upon 7 Frith Street, Soho (cited by Ware in 1756 as the plan form of the 'common house')

newel posts or from an effective handrail (Figure 4.4).

There is little doubt that the straightforward layout favoured by Gropius and Fry at the Benn Levy House, Chelsea (Figure 4.5), provides an inspirational example from the 1930s. The fine detailing in

steel, timber and glass has stood the test of time and illustrates the way generosity in plan gives rise to more comfortable proportions. The return landing at the base assists the spatial concept and shifts the main circulation from a collision with the open string. The open composition increases the spaciousness of the interior, unlike the traditional approach of infilling below the stairs with cupboards or a lavatory that brings the space back to corridor size. Another advantage in the detailing is the turned treads at the foot of the stair which divert the line towards the hallway.

4.2.2 Dog-legs

The dog-leg pattern is ideal for double-fronted variations (Figure 4.2c). It is also the basis of the 'London' plan that dates back to the 1660s.[2] This 'Universal' layout (Figure 4.3a) places dog-leg flights at the rear of the house so that all rooms are accessed from the common stairs. Variations in storey heights are accommodated by lengthening or by the use of winders. The ground floor usually has extended steps towards the entry passage,

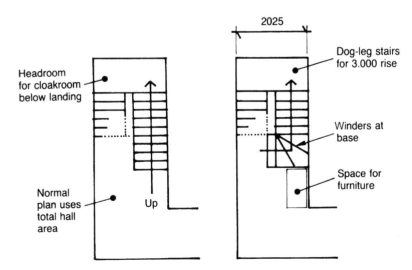

Figure 4.3b Turning stairs to improve a hallway. Reddington Road, 1870s, Architect: Philip Webb

Figure 4.4 Standard Danish Stair installed in the 'Marchesi' system built house (1981)

with the basement route neatly tucked in below. The visual aspect is comely, the best historic examples are probably the seventeenth-century pieces, constructed from oak, that still exist in the Inns of

Figure 4.5 Benn Levy House, Chelsea, 1935–6, Architects: Gropius and Fry

Court. Further consideration of stone and iron versions are given in Chapter 9.

Replacing the half landings with winders can reduce the floor opening to 1 800 mm × 1 600 mm (Figure 4.4). The area saved is added to the circulation space and ensures a wider range of options for locating doorways at all floor levels. Furniture handling on dog-leg stairs is not a problem provided that newel posts have been terminated close to the balustrade line. Similar stairs built within storey-height balustrades create insoluble problems for furniture removal. Another problem area is 'scissors' type stairs constructed within masonry shells, a popular method from the 1960s and 1970s for maisonettes in public housing. The central spine wall needs to be scalloped either end to give a turning circle for handling bulky furniture (Figure 4.6).

4.2.3 Domestic spiral and cylindrical stairs

The decorative and sculptural quality of spiral stairs is no doubt the reason that so many kits or standard spirals in concrete, steel or timber are now available. A contributing factor is the ease with which computer aids can speed designing such features to fulfil site requirements and to meet the onerous restrictions of the current Building Codes as given in Chapter 10. It is sufficient at this stage to confirm that 1 800 mm diameter is the minimum drum for spirals in private houses. This dimension assumes a clear headroom of 2 000 mm. The diameter can be reduced to 1 400 mm for a stair intended for occasional use with access to one room or a balcony etc. The normal diameters of 1 800 mm show no saving in well dimensions below minimal dog-legs

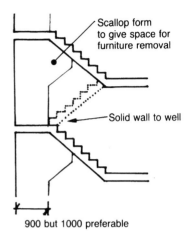

Scallop form
to give space for
furniture removal

Solid wall to well

900 but 1000 preferable

Figure 4.6 Scissors stair with scalloped spine walls

Figure 4.7 Domestic spiral stair, Highbury Terrace Mews, 1971, Architect: Peter Collymore (courtesy of Bill Toomey)

and winders. There is, however, the visual consideration where the spiral has a greater advantage (Figure 4.7) and the fact that the design cannot be compromised by boxing in for understairs cupboards or with lavatories for pygmies. The design problem has been greatly eased by standardized components and particularly those with threshold arrangements at each access point. Makers offer a range of riser proportions so that quarter

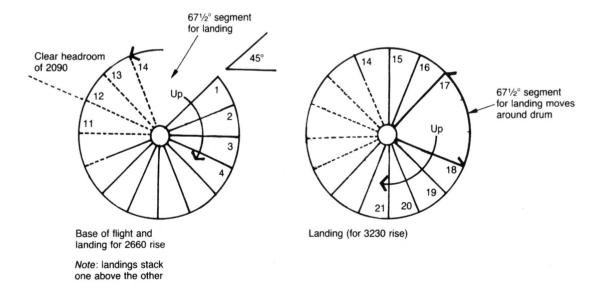

Figure 4.8 Landing locations

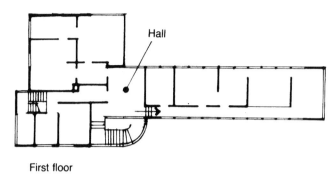

Figure 4.9a Shrublands, Chalfont St Giles, 1935, Architects: Mendelsohn and Chermayeff: First floor plan

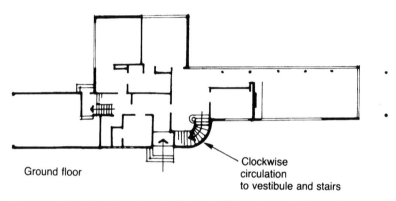

Figure 4.9b Shrublands, Chalfont St Giles: Ground floor plan

Figure 4.9c Shrublands, Chalfont St Giles: View of ground floor flight

landings can be neatly stacked one over the other to cover a choice of storey heights. Differing heights can be accomplished by adjusting landing locations (Figure 4.8). The easiest answer is to employ an open quadrant facing the main circulation that can be opened or closed according to the number of treads needed as this will produce a more consistent solution. Other methods involve turning the landing segment quarter by quarter where differences in storey height occur. The quarter landing shape makes for an easy transition from floor space to spiral geometry.

Cylindrical stairs have a more spacious effect whether placed free standing or within the shell of an enclosing drum. Contrasting the curved and straight line is a feature of early modernism. Mendelsohn and Chermayeff created a seminal house of the 1930s at Shrublands, Chalfont St Giles, where the swept line of the stair is placed at the crucial break in the plan (Figure 4.9). The elegance of the solution is extended into the detail of the swept platform at the base and to the helical handrail that terminates the balustrade. Another example of this genre is the work of Raymond McGrath at St Anne's Hill, Chertsey (Figure 4.10), where a segmental vestibule embraces a cantilever cylindrical stair. Such exercises in imagination raise expectations for the scenario at first floor. The Mendelsohn theme creates a fine hall with two-way views as well as access to the master suite and guest wing in descending order. McGrath's dramatic layout leads to the circular master bedroom that is the hub of the house, set in an eighteenth-century landscape garden.[3] Both these large houses were twin-stair designs, one for the master and one for the servants; the secondary stairs were mundane affairs tucked away in the corner of the plan. The social mores of the time dictated these concepts, though the circumstances at St Anne's Hill caused special conditions

Figure 4.10b St Anne's Hill, Chertsey: Hall and stairs

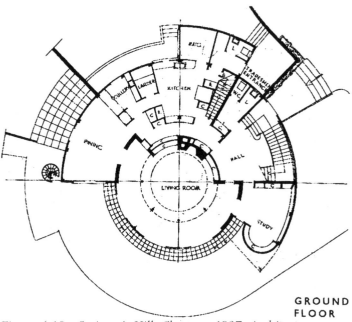

GROUND FLOOR

Figure 4.10a St Anne's Hill, Chertsey, 1937, Architect: Raymond McGrath: Ground floor plan

whereby the master bedroom had totally separate circulation from the servants. The origins for white concrete cylindrical stairs must surely be the creations of Le Corbusier and Pierre Jeanneret in their heroic period of the 1920s. The free-standing setting within the Villa Savoye raises the stair into the vantage point, with slots cut in the drum wall to reveal the building interior (Figure 4.11). The famous ramp is the ultimate pivotal zone which allows the whole space to unfold from ground floor to roof terrace. The structural role of stair drum or ramp framing is used to the full. Ernö Goldfinger borrowed the same theme for the half circular flight at Willow Road. Here the reinforced concrete floor slabs run cross wall to cross wall with an intermediate support on the reinforced concrete stair drum that is placed central to the depth of the plan (Figure 4.12).

4.2.4 Modernism and domestic stairs

The concept of the open stair within the open plan is the hallmark of the Corbusian ideal. The initial designs for the Dom-Ino Skeletal House (circa 1914–15) demon-

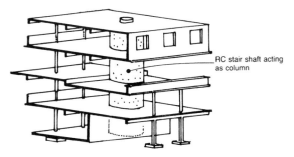

Figure 4.12 *Use of stair walls in structure, Willow Road, London, NW3, 1937, Architect: Ernö Goldfinger*

strated a framed structure with reinforced concrete dog-leg stairs spanning between cantilevered landing slabs (Figure 4.13*a*).[4] The development of this concept through the designs for Maison Citrohan arranged the stairs as direct flights to save frontage, with the final version built at the Weissenhof exhibition, Stuttgart, in 1927 (Figures 4.13*b* and 4.13*c*). The significance of these layouts is the way that dining and living areas are deployed as circulation zones without separation into rooms and stairhalls.

The modernist device is to use the stair as a freely-placed feature to liberate the spacial development of the interior. An example of this doctrine is the remodelling of a pair of houses in St Leonard's Terrace, Chelsea, by Richard Rogers Partnership. This design opens the traditional vertical box-like London home into a series of large horizontal spaces.

The major element is a double-height apartment at first floor with a projecting mezzanine forming a sleeping balcony. Access within the apartment is made via a staircase running on the diagonal (Figure 4.14). The use of the longer dimension for ascent increases the sense of space and enhances the fine proportions. The backdrop is a well-fenestrated façade comprising twelve windows. The

Figure 4.11 *Villa Savoye, 1929–31, Architects: Le Corbusier and Pierre Jeaneret. Stair and ramp*

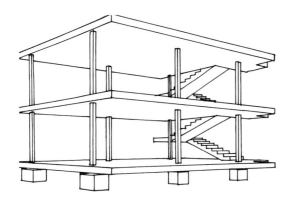

Figure 4.13a Dom-Ino Skeletal House: First sketch (circa 1914–15)

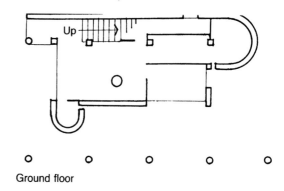

Ground floor

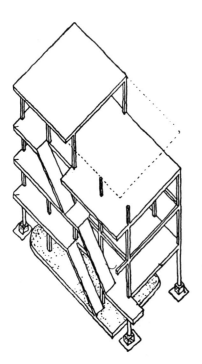

Figure 4.13b Frame for built example at Stuttgart, 1927, Architects: Le Corbusier and Pierre Jeanneret (from L'Architecture Vivante*)*

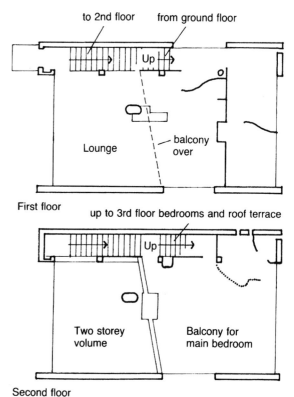

to 2nd floor   from ground floor

Lounge   balcony over

First floor

up to 3rd floor bedrooms and roof terrace

Two storey volume   Balcony for main bedroom

Second floor

Figure 4.13c Dom-Ino Skeletal House: Plan arrangements

conversion has a well-contrived subdivision between staff facilities at basement level, the grandparents' flat at ground floor and the children's territory zone at the upper levels, with the parental zone of the grand apartment sandwiched between. The principal vertical circulation, top to bottom, is a steel spiral stair-

case which rises in a self-contained well to bypass the principal living area. The subdivision allows for multiple use in the reverse order to the Goldfinger home which eventually accommodated three generations of the family floor by floor – the youngest family in the garden basement flat, Ernö and Ursula at ground

Figure 4.14 Rogers' Apartment, St Leonard's Terrace, London, 1985, Architects: Richard Rogers Partnership. General view of 2-storey volume with stair on diagonal

and first floor, whilst Grandma Goldfinger ruled the second floor.

The Hopkins house in Downshire Hill also shares the spacious quality of open planning, with the stair sited within the middle zone of a nine compartment plan. The planning grid is based upon a minimal steel framing module of 2×4 m. The core, that includes bathrooms and the spiral stair, is 2 m wide while the principal rooms towards the garden and street occupy a double bay of 4 m each (Figure 4.15*a*). The steel spiral forms a skeletal structure in a minimal tube within the main circulation space (Figure 4.15*b*). Flexibility in the layout allows partitions to be added as family requirements change, with the garden level split into flatlets when the children are older.

The thematic response can best be seen in the cantilever spiral that is at the heart of the Jencks Victorian villa. Here each tread fits one to the other like the spiralling of a conch shell. The depth and height are signified by a mosaic telling of the underworld set in the basement floor and by the cascading light from the domical 'eye' to the sky. Each step is numerated to tell of the ascent, the whole movement of the flight being captured by finely made sinuous handrailing. The oval plan is masterly, with spreadeagle treads that lead off into the landings (Figure 4.16).

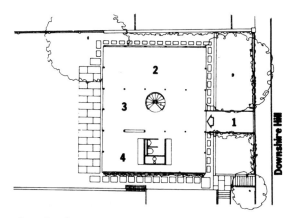

street level plan (scale 1:400)

key
1. footbridge
2. studio
3. sitting
4. sleeping
5. cooking
6. store
7. eating
8. games

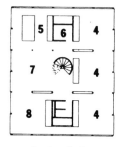

garden level plan

Figure 4.15a Hopkins House, Downshire Hill, London, 1976, Architects: Michael and Patty Hopkins: Layout plan

4.2.5 Ladders and steps

Ladders and steps are special forms of steeper design; they are permitted for particular purposes, e.g. occasional access to roof spaces or service rooms. Loft ladders are generally collapsible or operate with a trapdoor mechanism. The space limitations are the transverse run of the equipment within the roof for the extending pattern and the area needed when the ladder is erected, both the footspace and the girth needed to walk around the obstruction. Folding scissors ladders exist but these are not as stable as telescopic ladders.

Fixed steps have the advantage that access is permanent, with guard rails at the upper level; in addition non-mechanical items can fit site dimensions more easily. The summary of the British Regulations for long ladders is given in Figure 4.17. Half steps are also permitted, providing only one room is served, and are more comfortable to the tread than narrow rungs. In principle, ladders and half steps allow angles of ascent of between 60° and 70°. The construction of the latter can be made in pre-cast concrete, steel or

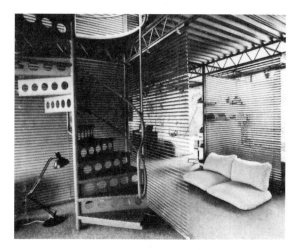

Figure 4.15b Hopkins House, Downshire Hill, London: General view of spiral stairs at core of plan

Figure 4.16 Stairs at the Jencks House, Ladbrooke, London, 1986, joint designer: Terry Farrell & Co.

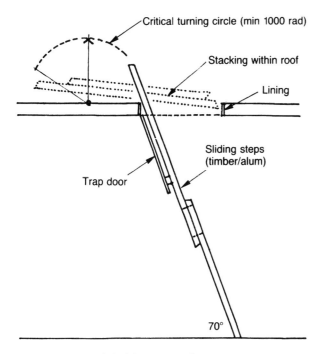

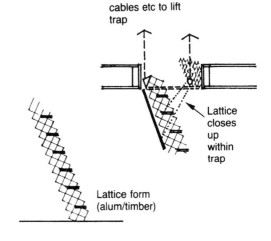

Figure 4.17 Loft ladder principles

timber; standard timber flights can be obtained from Denmark and Italy (Figure 4.18). For Building Regulations see Figure 10.1*d*.

4.2.6 Other forms

Three-turn forms take up more space than dog-leg or spirals. However, the openness of the central well can enhance the natural lighting given by the upper landing windows or roof lights. One source of these ideas is the vertical cores that served Ottoman domestic architecture. The structures are generally timber post and beam with brick infilling. The treads are often corbelled stone, braced by continuous newel framing. Wreathed handrails are replaced by panels of slats with individual handrails fitted between the verticals (Figure 4.19).

Figure 4.18 Proprietary ladder steps (courtesy of Space Saver Stairs (UK) Ltd)

Figure 4.19 Three-turn stairs: Ottoman Merchants House, Cairo (circa 1500)

Figure 4.20 Vertical or thermometer window featured in the rear elevation of the Winslow House, Chicago, 1893, Architect: Frank Lloyd Wright

4.2.7 Elevational considerations

Central siting for stairs or locations placed by internal walls provide no elevational problems apart from the provision of adequate windows to light the steps. Flights placed against the external wall look dramatic behind extensive glazing but make for difficulty with internal window cleaning (see Figure 4.9 to visualize the problems). Windows that step up with the flight may be the answer but often appear awkward externally. The vertical or thermometer window is the other dubious invention (Figure 4.20).

4.3 Stairs and lift cores in flats

4.3.1 Historic background

Dwellings stacked one above the other with staircases placed externally or internally reveal seminal layouts little altered by history. Multi-storey flats date back to Roman times. The remains at Ostia (Figure 4.21) reveal tenement structures that once rose five storeys, with access via internal passages and three-turn stairs to a similar pattern adopted by the Peabody Trust in London in the 1870s.

Open balcony access is used in Heriot's Hospital at Edinburgh (Figure 4.22*a*), with corner turrets and balconies to the courtyard. The form is also utilized in the development of the Old Town in seventeenth-century Edinburgh (Figure

Figure 4.21 Flats in Ostia (reconstruction)

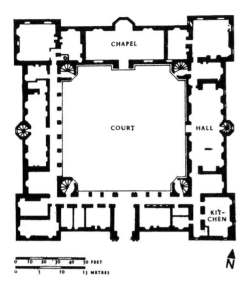

Figure 4.22a Balcony access and stairs in seventeenth-century Edinburgh: Plan of Heriot's Hospital, 1628 (from Summerson, J., Architecture in Britain 1530–1830, Penguin Books, 1991 © Yale University Press)

Figure 4.22b Typical tenements behind Royal Mile, Edinburgh (seventeenth century)

4.22*b*). The reasons for external approach probably relate to basic hygiene since the balconies or open stairs lead to privies in the outside walls as compared with more advanced Roman methods where a lucky few enjoyed bathrooms with water pipes fed from roof level aqueducts.[5] 'Walk-up' flats were eventually supplanted in the nineteenth century by multi-storey blocks served by hydraulic lifts within internal cores. Such construction was built exclusively for the middle and upper classes. London's first street of continental-style apartments was Victoria Street (laid out in 1852–71).[6] Typical plans of a 13-storey block show lift and main stairs for tenants with back stairs for servants and tradesmen.

The pattern of balcony access with common stairs dominated low-cost flatted housing in the UK and the Continent throughout the later nineteenth century right through to post-war construction after 1945. This was partly due to the economy of construction with the main stairs spaced as far apart as 48 m, serving perhaps eight flats at each landing.[7] Fire fighting was also easier to organize via external balconies and from staircases situated in the open air. Enthusiasts for balcony access would talk of constructing the social idea of 'streets in the sky'. The reality is often the most unpopular type of dwelling where privacy, quietness and safety is hard to come by, bedroom windows having to be placed overlooking the balconies. Idealists in the nineteenth century considered these dwellings far superior to the squalid terraced houses they replaced.

On the Continent a general pattern was to place gallery access flats around a large courtyard. The stairs are usually placed at the corners between the blocks which are entered via an entrance lodge at ground floor controlled by a concierge (Figure 4.23).

Direct access to all flats from a central core served by main stairs, lift and secondary fire stairs (if needed) is easier to manage (refer to Figures 4.24*a–b*). Such arrangements have the advantage that noise can be isolated from the quieter zones of the surrounding dwellings.

4.3.2 Generic forms

A generic analysis is given in Figure 4.24, the basic subdivision between single and

Figure 4.23 Nineteenth-century flats in Budapest on the Familistere pattern, with balcony access and corner stairs

double staircase forms depending upon fire brigade requirements. There must be direct fire service access to a staircase via a window or balcony point. The lobby is the common method of separate downward escape from the risk of smoke (burning flats or refuse ducts). Tall flats (above brigade ladder height) are often devised with continuous balcony fronts and external steps to ensure that escape from each dwelling can be safely made via an open air route to an assembly point, which is reachable by brigade equipment. More detailed consideration of means of escape in the case of flats as well as individual dwellings is provided in Chapter 10.

Fire insurance preclude spiral forms so that direct flights, dog-legs or three-turn stairs are the most common forms. Lifts, in case of fire, are often reserved for fire fighters, which implies that the lift cage is separate and no longer enclosed by three-turn stairs (as Figure 4.24*b*). Such enclosure was a popular economic form devised in the last century. Separating the lift from stairs has the advantage that 'through lift' access is feasible, giving considerable benefit when planning for pram or wheelchair use.

The 'scissors' plan based on a central corridor serving at least three floors followed the design of Le Corbusier at Unité d'Habitation, Marseilles, in 1950 (Figure 4.25)[8]. From the central street, flats are entered left and right. You either entered the living room area and went up to the bedrooms, or onto the bedroom balcony and down to the living room and further bedrooms. Thus the living rooms with the two-storey balconies face either side of the block. The building should therefore be placed east–west to give sunlight to all living rooms part of the day. Darbourne and

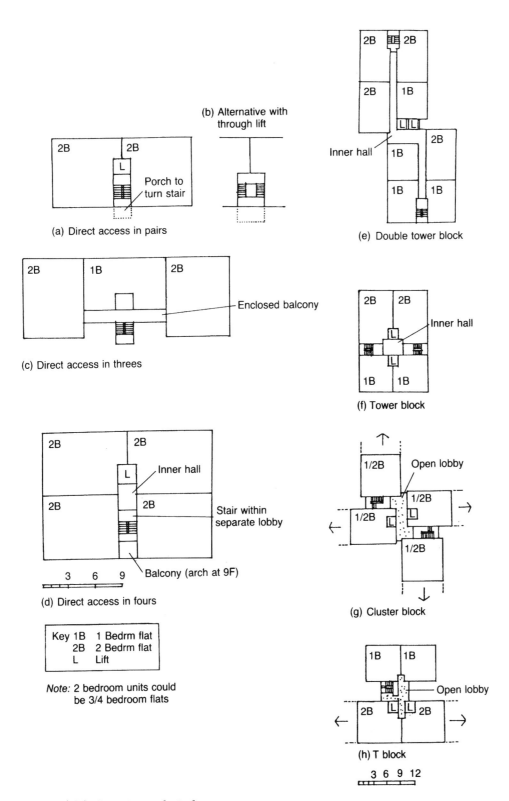

Figure 4.24 Generic analysis for access cores

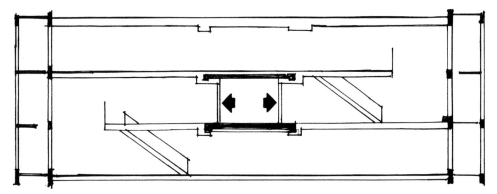

Figure 4.25 Unité d'Habitation, Marseilles, Le Corbusier

Darke adopted the design in the flats at Lillington Gardens in 1963 (Figure 4.26). The flats were planned to give most flats living room aspect on one side, bedrooms on the other, thus enabling the blocks to be placed north–south as well. This also allows for the noisy areas, the living rooms, to be placed one over another and the quiet areas, the bedrooms, likewise.

4.3.3 Preferred tread-to-rise dimensions

A few words are needed on preferred tread-to-rise relationships. Ideally a com-mon stair proportion should be used throughout a residential scheme, say 190 mm rise × 240 mm going for both common and private stairs.

The British Regulations are, however, being continually revised, the latest revision being in 1998. These are dealt with in detail in Chapter 10. It is sufficient here to state that for private stairs the maximum rise permitted is 220 mm, with a minimum going also of 220 mm and a maximum pitch of 42°. A comfortable proportion is 190 mm rise × 240 mm going. The timber trade offer a standard stair as noted in Section 4.1. For institutional buildings a

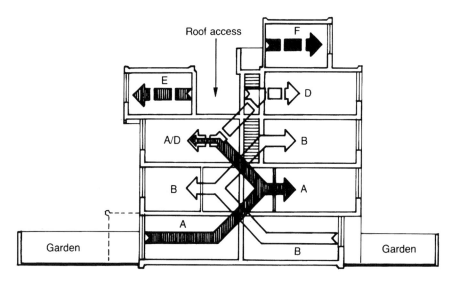

Figure 4.26 Scissors-type stairs at Lillington Gardens, 1963–71, Architects: Darborne and Darke: plan and section (see Figure 4.6 for detailed section through stairs)

shallower pitch is required, with the rise being a maximum of 180 mm and the going a minimum of 280 mm. In both cases the formula adopted is twice the rise plus the going to equal not more than 700 mm or less than 550 mm. Under access for the disabled regulations, a lift should be provided to serve the living rooms on all floors, but if this is not possible the common stair has to be reduced to give a maximum rise of 170 mm to help the old and infirm.

4.3.4 Elevational considerations

Reference to the generic forms in Figure 4.24 demonstrates the basic dilemma, namely to plan arrangements that permit maximum fenestration to the flat units. For example in Figure 4.24, plan (a) would provide a two window elevation while plans (g) and (h) can provide three.

Internal staircases arranged to meet fire brigade needs will present the easiest solution with top lighting provided for daytime requirements. Reference to Maison Clarté (Figure 7.5d) reveals the way central stairs designed with glass treads can permit a rooflight to filter daylight down through eight storeys.

Stair shafts placed externally to the building volume become towers whether lightly framed or faced in solid materials (refer back to Figures 4.22a and 4.22b). In long slab blocks, external towers can break up the building into identifiable elements (Figure 4.27a). It is a matter of scale, however, since the same concept applied to tall flats, say twelve or more storeys, increases the sense of megalomania.

Stair and lift cores placed as nodal elements between flats have the advantage that shading will not occur and can enable

Figure 4.27a Staircase fenestration in flats: Identification elements: Fasenenplatz, Berlin, 1984, Architect: Gotfried Bohm

a more subtle contrast to be achieved between the domestic and staircase fenestration (Figure 4.27b). In this example the stair windows relate in cill height to half landings on the flights and can be quite different in size to the windows of the habitable rooms. The stair which links two blocks often takes the form of a glazed link (Figure 4.27c).

Other treatments evolve from the profile of staircase enclosures brought across the façade. For the Aalto designed dormitories at Cambridge (Massachusetts) for MIT, this feature is on the accessible face of their designs (Figure 4.27d).

Another version is the courtyard plan of Harvey Court, Cambridge, by Sir Leslie

Figure 4.27b Staircase fenestration in flats: Britz Siedlung, Berlin, 1931, Architect: Bruno Taut

Figure 4.27c Staircase fenestration in flats: Bellahoj, Copenhagen, 1954, Architect: A. S. Dominia

Martin, where the stairs climb parallel to the block. The underside of the ziggurat form permitting the flights to infill the colonnade can be expressed as part of the elevation (Figure 4.27*e*).

Combining the entry arrangements to flats with refuse chutes is one of the more obnoxious ideas in British housing policy and particularly where the terminating chute and communal dustbin has to occur close by the ground floor hallway. Basement servicing for refuse is commonplace in continental Europe and the USA and explains why flat entries and stairs from abroad have been chosen for the final illustrations.

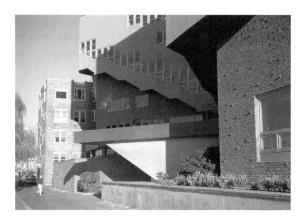

Figure 4.27d Staircase fenestration in flats: Baker House Dormitory, Cambridge MA, 1948, Architect: Alvar Aalto

Figure 4.27e Staircase fenestration in flats: Harvey Court, Cambridge, 1962, Architects: Sir Leslie Martin and Colin St. John Wilson

References

1   Generic plans – a term developed by the former GLC and Ministry of Housing. Both organizations published 'preferred plans' upon the generic basis. Useful references are *Space in the Home*, DOE, HMSO, 1969 and *Metric House Shells*, NBA, 1969.

2   It is difficult to pin down the source of the 'London' house plan but John Summerson in *Georgian London* (Pleiades Books, 1945) recognizes that Nicholas Barbon was the first speculator to build this pattern of house extensively after the Fire of London. The construc-tional method with brick envelope walls to a studwork interior was standard practice until 1914.

3   St Anne's Hill – the eighteenth-century landscape garden was created by Walpole, the focus being the semicircular portico recaptured by Raymond McGrath in the modern house in 1935–6. For details refer to Christopher Tunnard's book *Gardens in the Modern Landscape*, 1938.

4   Dom-Ino Skeletal House – original design patented by Le Corbusier and Max du Bois in 1914.

5.   Roman drainage – the lucky few in Ostia or Rome enjoyed water-borne drainage, namely those occupying buildings built close by or below an aqueduct structure. Refer to p. 22, *Everyday Life in Ancient Rome* by F. R. Cowell (BT Batsford & G P Putman and Son, 1961).

6   Mansion flats – Donald J. Olsen describes mid-nineteenth century flats of London in *The Growth of Victorian London* (BT Batsford Ltd, 1976), Chapter 3, 'Blocks of Flats' (pp. 114–18).

7   Balcony access stairs – the notes are taken from the Ministry of Health Housing Manual 1949, but by then the MOH were saying that under some circumstances balconies might be of any length.

8   Post-Le Corbusier version central passage – refer to layouts for Unité d'Habitation, Marseilles, 1945, in *Oeuvre Complet 1938–46*.

5 External stairs

5.1 Garden architecture

Some aspects of designing external stairs come within the realm of garden architecture. It is not possible to condense that vast topic, the reader is therefore left to search out their favoured source, Oriental or Islamic, English, French, Italian or Spanish or perhaps that blend of vernacular that pertains to European landscape design today.[1]

There are common forms of external steps. A primary role concerns steps that relate to buildings, a secondary aspect are those which serve the functional needs for access into or through the landscape or townscape. Both forms have developed a decorative role in garden architecture, like steps placed around a pool or else in a kerb, or plinths to mark differing levels, and the decorative aspect can be enhanced by the use of materials, such as grass versus paving.

External stairs carry symbolic undertones with perhaps a greater poignancy due to the connection with nature. There are many temples of the Buddhist faith that are constructed in the form of steps to heaven (Figure 2.1a).

The reverence inspired by a temple mount can also pertain to more modest themes, as witnessed by the Kennedy Memorial, Runnymede, for it demonstrates the most eloquent expression of steps and surfaces in a simple landscape setting. The approach is through woodland with the pathway picked out in granite setts, the steeper parts having ramped steps. The open meadow beyond the wood has mounded setts that rise to the climax of the memorial. The formal approach route is made via sunken stone treads of ample proportion, these relating to the terrace paving on which is mounted the plinth block and memorial stone (Figures 5.1a and 5.1b).

A differing response occurs with steps that lead down into sunken chambers or that disappear below water. The psychology of descent into shade or below ground or below water is totally opposite to the optimism in climbing Tai Shan. Some significant examples are the cistern temples in India where the architectural ensemble is a preparation for the ceremonial cleansing at the lowest level. The cisterns and water steps featured in many temple complexes are designed for large crowds of worshippers within a sacred enclosure (Figure 5.2a).

The theme of descent and purification was captured superbly at the Memorial de la Déportation at the eastern end of the Ile de la Cité, in Paris (Figure 5.2b). Here one descends from a green garden down stone steps into a sunken shaded courtyard of masonry and iron with glimpsed views of the Seine forever breaking past the promontory; turn round and there is the inner sanctuary, a peaceful softly lit hall of remembrance. The return route is back into the light and the hustle and bustle of the market behind Notre Dame.

Figure 5.1a Kennedy Memorial, Runnymede, 1965, Architect: Sir Geoffrey Jellicoe: Ramped steps

Figure 5.1b Kennedy Memorial, Runnymede: Formal steps and memorial

Figure 5.2a Water steps and tank, Temple at Chidambaram, India (Courtesy of Timothy Blanc)

Figure 5.2b Memorial de la Déportation, Paris, 1962, sculpture by Desserprit, Architect: Georges-Henri Pingusson

5.2 Historic precedent

The outdoor room is probably the most pertinent description that holds true for the vernacular English garden.[2] The precedent stretches back in European terms to the Italian Renaissance and in turn to the gardens created in Southern Spain at Granada and Seville. In essence, the outdoor space is compartmented into 'rooms and passages' laid out across sloping land with stairs to facilitate movement from level to level.

Stepped paths are matched with stepped parapets in Granada (Figure 5.3a) in contrast to pebble ramps enlivened by fountains bordered by walls having waterfall copings (Figure 5.3b). Spanish gardeners accompanied the Borgias when they went to live in Italy; little wonder therefore that the stepped water gardens in Tuscany, Rome, and its hinterland or Venetia have the qualities of Andalusia.

The quintessence must surely exist in the terraced and multi-staired water paradise at the rear of the Villa d'Este (Figure 5.4a). This garden, which serves as an outdoor room, is the size of Trafalgar Square and criss-crossed with three vistas in each direction, with ramps and staircases that tumble down 20 m from the palace to the furthest terrace. Each step and turn is water embel-

Figure 5.3a Moorish inspiration in the Generalife Gardens, Granada, fifteenth century: restored in 1920s: Stepped paths and parapets

Figure 5.3b Pebble ramps, enlivened by fountains bordered by walls having waterfall copings

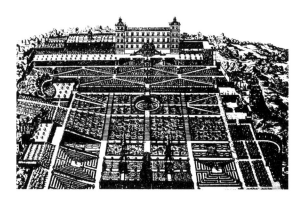

Figure 5.4a Villa d'Este, Tivoli, 1550s, designer: Pierre Ligorio: Key plan

lished (Figures 5.4*b* and 5.4*c*). Plans of the Spanish Steps in Rome (Figures 5.5*a* and 5.5*b*) convey in their arabesques and curves the notion of a musical cadence. The concept of turning, stopping, advancing and retreating is the key to the elaboration achieved within this Italian tradition. The symbol of dance and lovers' meetings is captured by the sublime music of *Le Nozze di Figaro* where the penultimate scene occurs within an Italian garden.

A similar cadence occurs at Villa Garzoni where designers have translated the outdoor space into a veritable palace of garden rooms with some of the grandest external stairs ever constructed (Figure 5.6).[3] The key visual element in Italian gardens is the role played by stairs as scenery to frame the views and where the diagonal or curving balustrade patterns provide the essential clues as to direction and geometrical composition. The landscape proportion of riser to tread is often as gentle as

Figure 5.4b Villa d'Este, Tivoli: Return stairs enclosing a fountain

Figure 5.4c Villa d'Este, Tivoli: Stepped ramp, waterfall coping and gargoyle

100 mm × 400 mm as occurs in the Spanish Steps (Figure 5.5c). Landscape architects are taught to use a different proportion from interior designers, usually twice the rise plus the tread to equal 700 mm instead of 600 mm.

Another detail of Italianate design is the way the spatial experience is played upon or pinched at stair locations (Figures 5.7a–f). Perspective effect can be increased by tapering the flight or by reducing the balustrade size in distant views. Expectations can be raised by using curved platform steps at gateways either sunken or raised flights, a favourite device of Edwin Lutyens. Dull, repetitive parallel treads can be

enhanced by slightly curving the nosing edge (in plan), a detail referred to by Sir George Sitwell in his treatise *On the Making of Gardens* (Figure 5.7e) illustrates a curved nosing line taken from the terrace steps at Renishaw. The use of a footspace at the base and head of garden steps will prevent wear and tear in a lawn setting, the geometry of this footspace also assisting with orientation.

Aalto devised a feature of lawn steps for his civic buildings in Finland. Figure 5.8 illustrates the rear of the Town Hall in Seinajoki.

5.3 Steps outside buildings

Returning to mundane matters, the National Building Regulations in Britain call for ground floors to be at least 150 mm above the natural exterior level, hence a step is needed at all entries (Figure 5.9a) or else a ramped pavement where disabled access is mandatory (Figure 5.9b). The 1998 National Building Regulations call for textured pavings at ramps to identify such features for the blind and partially sighted. Both elements can be combined in a single design (Figure 5.9c). The dimensions of the basic form should be in scale with the door, which now has to be wide enough for a wheelchair, the depth should be a comfortable footspace.

Providing a flight of steps by external doors needs to take into account safety of egress, space for door swings and a walking distance before the first riser, say a distance of 1800 mm minimum (Figure 5.10a). Balustrade protection should be given to both sides or handrails

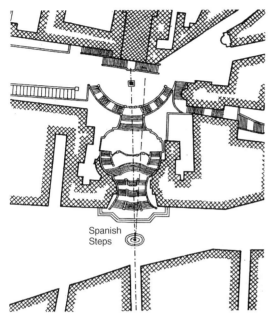

Figure 5.5c Spanish Steps, Rome: Detail of gentle riser-to-tread proportion

Figure 5.5a Spanish Steps, Rome, 1721–3, designer: Francesco de Sanctis: Key plan (from Schuster, F., Treppen, *Hoffman Verlag, 1949)*

provided where the platform category of stairs is employed. Balustrading constructed with tubular steel can incorporate electrical conduit and lighting systems placed within the handrail profile. In many European countries ramp blocks are built into the flight (Figure 5.10*b*),

Figure 5.5b Spanish Steps, Rome: General view

Figure 5.6 A veritable palace of garden rooms: Villa Garzoni, Collodi, 1652

but in Britain ramped circulation has to follow a defined slope of given width (refer to the Building Regulations regarding the disabled in Chapter 10). The imposing civic entrance to the Law Courts in Vancouver is a very successful application of these principles on a monumental scale, the complex levels combining a sitting out area with diagonal ramps and stairs for ceremonial purposes (Figures 5.10c and 5.10d). The concept relates to platform steps employed in pyramid form with both external and internal corners. The main advantage is the prominence that such forms give to entries (Figures 5.11a and 5.11b). Direct flights of stairs are more practical and easier to adapt for safety with guard rails and perimeter balustrading (Figure 5.11c) and with ramps accommodated alongside. Direct

flights can also be devised to handle vast crowds of people, as in the layout of sports stadia. In these circumstances the steps are divided into passageways of 1 800 mm widths separated by engineered guard rails, with groups of stairs limited to 16 risers between landings;[4] failure can produce a catastrophe (Figure 5.11d). In Britain, such stairs have to break their alignment at every third landing. Similar provisos exist when designing the approaches to pedestrian bridges or underpasses, the customary layout having a choice of stairs and ramps.

Reverting to simple steps placed by building entries, there are severe constructional restraints that affect the design solution. By illustration, the plinth or block of steps can be made as a ground slab independent of the building mass (Figure

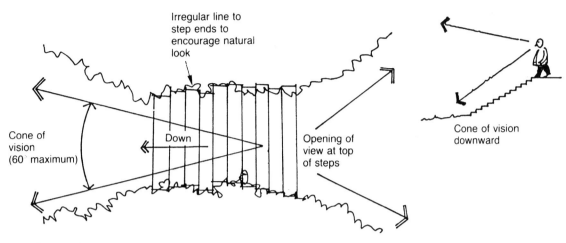

Irregular line to
step ends to
encourage natural
look

Cone of vision
downward

Cone of
vision
(60° maximum)

Down

Opening of
view at top
of steps

Note: Contrast between downward
and upward views

Figure 5.7a Italianate detail: Tapered layout for perspective effect

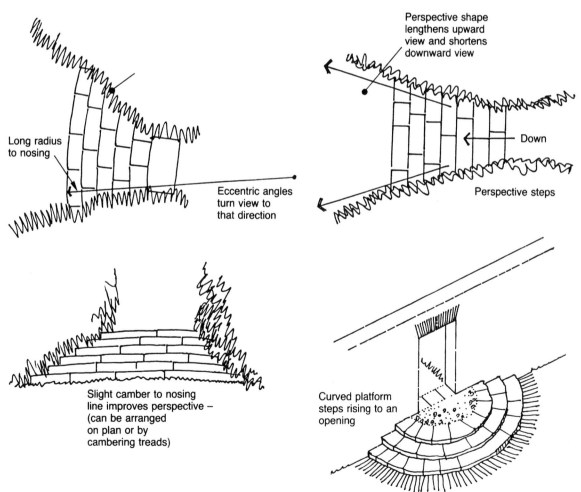

Perspective shape
lengthens upward
view and shortens
downward view

Long radius
to nosing

Eccentric angles
turn view to
that direction

Down

Perspective steps

Slight camber to nosing
line improves perspective –
(can be arranged
on plan or by
cambering treads)

Curved platform
steps rising to an
opening

*Figure 5.7b Italiante detail: Pinched space at stair
location*

Figure 5.7c Italiante detail: Curved platform steps

Figure 5.7d Italiante detail: Differing heights of balustrade to give greater distance, Powys Castle (date unknown)

Figure 5.7e Italiante detail: Curved line of tread to improve visual effect. Renishaw, 1990s, designer: Sir George Sitwell

5.12*a*), or else as a cantilever extension of the ground floor slab or adjacent wall (Figure 5.12*b*). The other concepts involve independent framing in steel or timber (Figures 5.12*c* and 5.12*d*).

5.4 Steps in landscape

The most extensive ramped and stepped construction ever made is the roadway which surmounts the Great Wall of China (Figure 5.13*a*), the only human construction said to be visible from the Moon. The design embraces a defensive wall, backed by a 4.5 m paved surface, either ramped or set out as stepped ramps in the steeper sections. The materials employed are largely brickwork. The undulating lengths involve all forms of inclined surfaces, ramps, zig zag climbs, curved and wide spaced steps, a source of ideas for every other form of hilly path in the landscape (Figure 5.13*b*).

The conversion of private gardens into a public domain can cause problems – not least the lack of guard rails, as seen at Lindisfarne Castle now owned by the National Trust (Figure 5.14). At present this detail is covered by a warning notice and adequate insurance. Matters were just as problematical after Lutyens' improvements had been completed in 1908. The following quotation is from a letter to his wife, Lady Emily concerning a visit by the Prince of Wales (later King George V). The Prince 'was terribly alarmed at the gangways up and wanted a wall built. I told him we had pulled one down and that if he really thought it unsafe we would put nets out. He thought that very funny'.

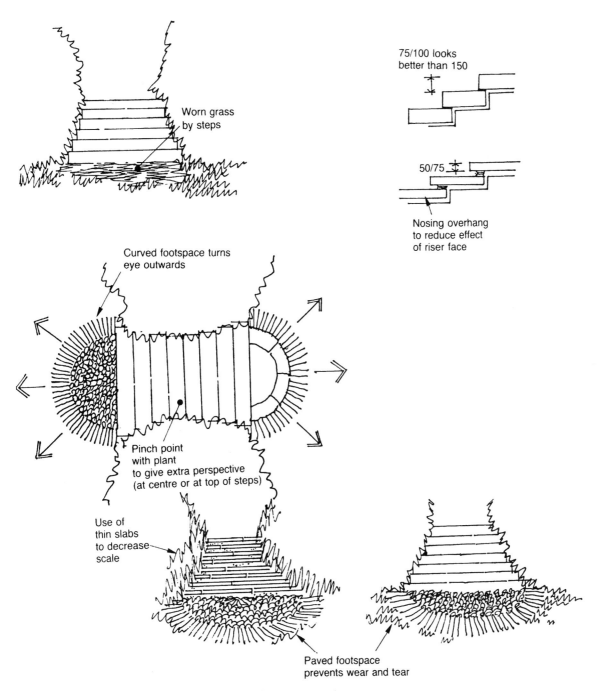

Worn grass by steps

75/100 looks better than 150

50/75

Nosing overhang to reduce effect of riser face

Curved footspace turns eye outwards

Pinch point with plant to give extra perspective (at centre or at top of steps)

Use of thin slabs to decrease scale

Paved footspace prevents wear and tear

Figure 5.7f Italiante detail: Footspace in relation to garden steps

Figure 5.8 Grass steps, Town Hall, Seinajoki, Finland (Alva Aalto)

Monumental steps in landscape are usually associated with Baroque grandeur: Caserta, Chatsworth and Versailles are illustrated as typical (Figure 5.15*a–c*). The main vista at Caserta is almost a mile in length, constructed as a canal with waterfalls and water steps decorated by fountains and sculpture. It is certainly inspired by Grillet's cascade at Chatsworth, a fraction of the scale deployed at Caserta but still faithfully capturing the delight of water steps as an

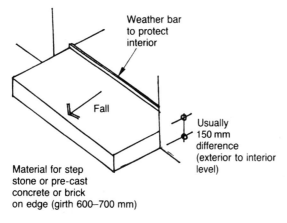

Figure 5.9a Simple steps outside buildings: Basic form of door step

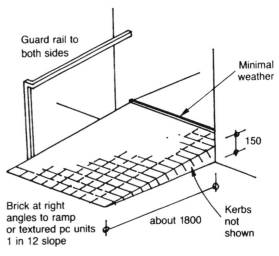

Figure 5.9b Basic ramped entry

Figure 5.9c Combined pattern. New entry steps at RIBA HQ, London, 1980s, Architect: J. Carey

umbilical thread in landscape (Figure 5.15*b*).

The Sun King's domain portrayed by the park at Versailles has within it the symbolic elements of the state, the farm, forest, lake, river and the city, represented by the enfolding wings of the royal palace. The terraces provide a vast dais as to a throne, the edges become castle walls broken by vast stairs that open the view to the horizon (Figure 5.15*c*). The detail that links each parterre within the 'dais' are kerb pro-

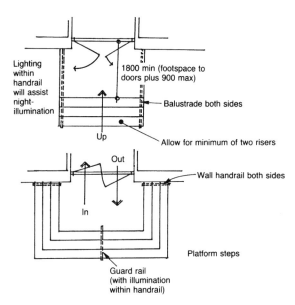

Figure 5.10a Direct flight steps: Basic dimensions

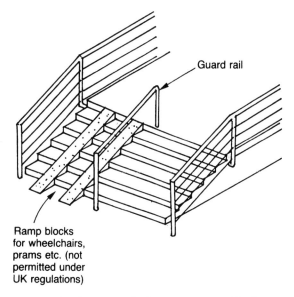

Figure 5.10b Direct flight steps: Ramp blocks

files that match the treads and risers to the terrace steps and in turn to the plinth mould of the Palace of Versailles (Figure 5.15*d*). A superb monumental detail of steps in landscape architecture.

5.5 Steps in townscape

Town planning has always been important in creating a space where changes in levels play an important part – the Romans in their forums of ancient times, the Renaissance with piazzas such as the Capitol, Rome (Figure 2.17), or the Spanish Steps (Figure 5.5). The opposite can be said of the narrow steps found in Italian hill towns or Cornish fishing ports (Figures 5.16*a* and 5.16*b*) where surprise views are obtained at each change of direction.

Today pedestrianization of our city centres has given us some excellent civic spaces, notably through the work of Lawrence Halprin as part of a pedestrian network within the cities of Portland and

Figure 5.10c General view, ceremonial stairs and ramps at the Courts Complex, Vancouver, 1972–9, Architect: Arthur Erickson

Figure 5.10d Direct flight steps: Detail view

Figure 5.11a Platform steps and large-scale stairs: Semicircular form, Mausoleum of the Aga Khan, Aswan, Egypt

Figure 5.11b Splayed form at entry to Federal offices, Seattle, USA, 1974, Landscape Architect: Richard Haag

Seattle. The Portland plan comprises a link between the university area and the civic buildings and the edge of 'downtown'. A plaza has been created at either end of the walkway route, where steps play a major role in the urban landscape (Figure 5.17*a*). Halprin has woven together the movement patterns around Lovejoy Plaza with space for water and a gazebo with ramps placed around the edge of the space to enable full participation by the community (Figure 5.17*b*).

Finally, at Broad Street, Arup Associates have created London's first new square. The central feature is a round banked auditorium where promotions are held and in the winter the whole central area is frozen over for skating. In summer office workers use the area like a park to eat their sandwiches and relax in the sun (Figure 5.18).

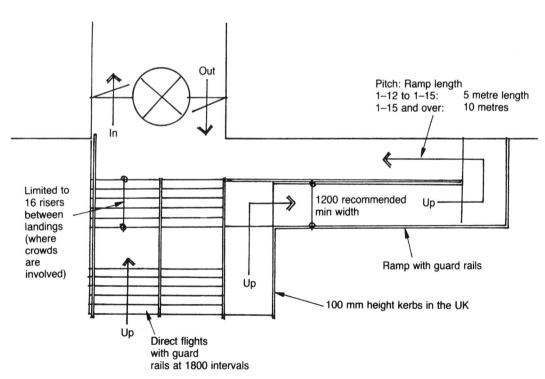

Figure 5.11c Use of guard rails and balustrades for direct stairs and ramps at entries

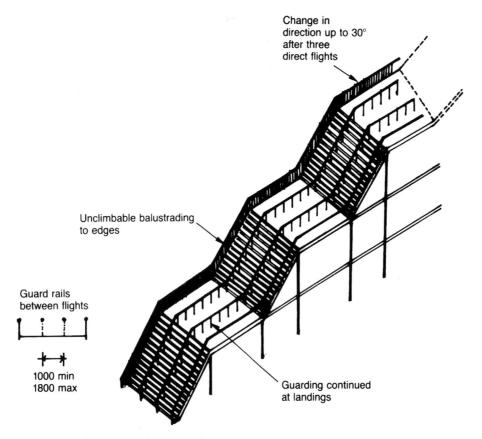

Change in
direction up to 30°
after three
direct flights

Unclimbable balustrading
to edges

Guard rails
between flights

1000 min
1800 max

Guarding continued
at landings

Figure 5.11d Large-scale external stairs in sports stadia

*Figure 5.12a Constructional restraints upon
design: Independent slab steps*

Figure 5.12b Cantilever slab stairs

Figure 5.12d Stair platform in timber

Figure 5.12c Stair platform in steel

Figure 5.13a The Great Wall of China (221–210 BC)

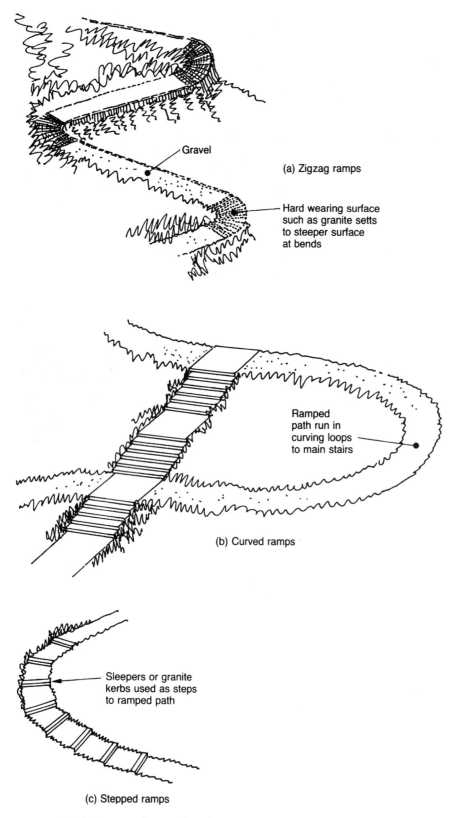

Gravel

(a) Zigzag ramps

Hard wearing surface
such as granite setts
to steeper surface
at bends

Ramped
path run in
curving loops
to main stairs

(b) Curved ramps

Sleepers or granite
kerbs used as steps
to ramped path

(c) Stepped ramps

Figure 5.13b Forms of stepped paths

Figure 5.14 Stepped ramp, Lindisfarne Castle,
1911, Sir Edwin Lutyens

Figure 5.15a Palozzo Reale, Caserta, 1752,
designer, Vanvitelli: detail of water steps

Figure 5.15b Water steps, Chatsworth, Derbyshire, 1694, Architect: Grillet (pupil of Le Notre)

Figure 5.15c Great staircase, Versailles, 1661–81, designer: Le Notre

Figure 5.15d Detail of plinths and steps

Figure 5.16a Steps in townscape: Prague, Czech Republic

Figure 5.16b Detail of steps at Portmerion, 1920s, Architect: Sir Clough Williams-Ellis

Figure 5.17a Pedestrian area, Lovejoy Plaza, Portland, Oregon, 1967–8 (Lawrence Halprin)

Figure 5.17b Detail of steps, Plaza, Portland

Figure 5.18 New outdoor plaza with stepped arena, Broadgate (Arup Associates)

References

1   Garden history and garden design – further reading: There is no shortage of books and guides to stimulate ideas; the following selection are those which are best documented concerning garden steps.
    Oriental. *The Chinese Garden* by Maggie Keswick (Academy Editions, 1978).
    Spanish. *Spanish Gardens* by Marquesa de Casa Valdes (Antique Collectors' Club, 1987).
    English. *Houses & Gardens by E. L. Lutyens* by Lawrence Weaver (Country Life, 1913).
    French. *The French Garden 1500–1800* by W. H. Adams (New York, 1979).
    American. *Lawrence Halprin*, published as Volume No. 4 by Process 1978.
    General Reference. *Landscape of Man* by Geoffrey and Susan Jellicoe (Thames & Hudson, 1975). *Modern Garden* by Peter Shepherd (The Architectural Press, 1953).

2   *The Edwardian Garden* by David Ottewill (Yale University Press, 1989).

3   Refer to descriptions of Italian gardens in the following: *Italian Gardens of the Renaissance* by J. C. Shepherd and G. A. Jellicoe (Princeton, Architectural Press, 1986). *Italian Gardens* by Georgina Masson (Thames & Hudson, 1987).

4   For strength of guard rails refer to Chapter 10.

6 Detailed construction: timber

The intention is to look at constructional ideas rather than the 'hands on' approach inherited from the nineteenth century where every method of setting out raking treads or wreathing to handrails is portrayed.[1] There are many excellent carpenters' manuals that provide this back-up today, reinforced by computer-aided design (CAD) packages used by designers and manufacturers. Figures 6.1a–d are intended as a reminder of the tactile quality associated with timber stairs: an explanation is given in Section 6.7 for the selection made.

Figure 6.1b The ultimate in timber elaboration. The main stairs at the Gamble House, Pasadena (balustrade modelled on the 'lifting cloud' motif of Japan), 1908, Architects: Henry and Charles Greene

6.1 Framing

The most primitive stairs relied on footholds chopped into a log, the next stage was the ladder form, still used in adventure playgrounds (Figures 6.2a and 6.2b). Robust treads can be cut from quartered

Figure 6.1a Ladder steps made from planks, circa twelfth century, Norway

logs and secured down to a carriage timber. Ships' ladders reveal considerable refinement with members whittled down to give the most efficient use of timber. Such construction is the prototype of today's open tread stairs (Figure 6.2c). The stability relies on effectively connecting the outer strings in the absence of overlapping rungs or treads of the more primitive pattern. The essential elements can be summarized as follows:

- Uncut strings to maximize longitudinal strength.
- solid plank or multi-ply treads with adequate glue line to mortices.
- Steel cross ties with plate bolt ends to tie the strings together.
- Refinements such as part risers will assist with the load-bearing quality of the treads. This will increase the glue-line and help comply with the National

Figure 6.1c Elegant wooden flight reinforced by a wrought iron flitch within the strings (late eighteenth century), Stamford Assembly Rooms

Figure 6.1d Spiral stairs, called the Miraculous Stairs, built without nails, 1878, Our Lady of Light Chapel, Sante Fe, New Mexico

Building Regulations concerning the maximum 100 mm gap.

The width-to-span proportions are dictated by engineering and the economics of timber supply. Open tread flights are usually limited to a metre width and for runs up to 16 risers. The sizings given in Figure 6.2c are for domestic purposes, say 900 mm width × 14 risers.

Wider designs, up to 1 800 mm, will involve carriage pieces with cantilever treads or a combination with steel brackets to fully support long span treads, shown in Figure 6.2d. Cut-string open stairs appear clumsy and present problems in effectively framing treads and

Figure 6.2a Framing timber stairs: Log pole with footholds chopped out, circa twelfth century, Norway

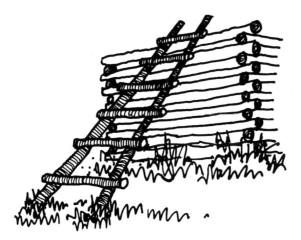

Figure 6.2b Framing timber stairs: Log ladder, circa twentieth century, children's playground

strings; such construction is more appropriate to composite assemblies. Narrow ladder-like steps are permitted in the UK for access to a single room, see Section 4.2.5 for details. Conventional framing relies on 'box construction' where a set of stairs is 'cased' together, hence the term 'staircase'. Mass production and preferred dimensions have ensured that costs are well below custom-made designs. Staircase kits from suppliers include a range of modules that come with all the ancillary details – newels, balustrades, handrailing and trim for platform treads and return nosings where cut strings are preferred. It is also possible to directly assemble dog-leg and multiple-turn flights from standard components. Figure 6.3 is a typical page from a manufacturer's catalogue.[2] Compare that to the superior quality of profile where an experienced architect is involved, as with the replacement stair in Figure 6.4b. The newel post has a framing role in

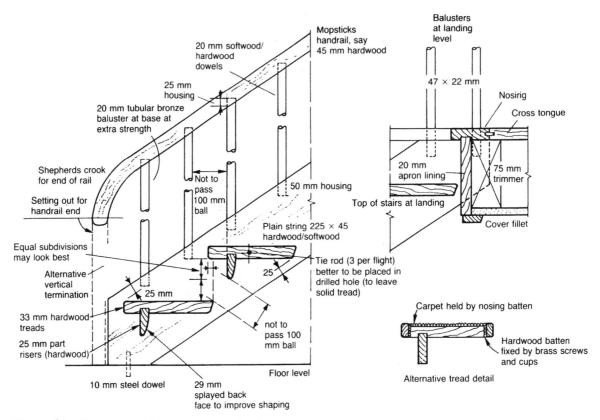

Figure 6.2c Framing timber stairs: Details of open tread stairs

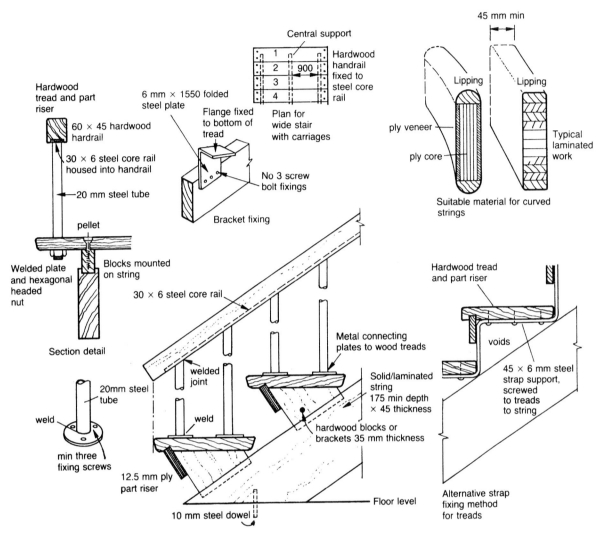

Central support

1		
2	900	
3		
4		

Plan for
wide stair
with carriages

Hardwood
handrail
fixed to
steel core
rail

Hardwood
tread and part
riser

60 × 45 hardwood
hardrail

30 × 6 steel core rail
housed into handrail

20 mm steel tube

pellet

Welded plate
and hexagonal
headed
nut

Section detail

6 mm × 1550 folded
steel plate

Flange fixed
to bottom of
tread

No 3 screw
bolt fixings

Bracket fixing

45 mm min

Lipping   Lipping

ply veneer

ply core

Typical
laminated
work

Suitable material for curved
strings

Blocks mounted
on string

30 × 6 steel core rail

welded
joint

20mm steel
tube

weld

weld

min three
fixing screws

12.5 mm ply
part riser

10 mm steel dowel

Metal connecting
plates to wood treads

Solid/laminated
string
175 min depth
× 45 thickness

hardwood blocks or
brackets 35 mm thickness

Floor level

Hardwood tread
and part riser

voids

45 × 6 mm steel
strap support,
screwed
to treads
to string

Alternative strap
fixing method
for treads

Figure 6.2d Framing timber stairs: Open treads with carriage pieces

conventional wood-framed stairs, it provides a bearing plane for flights and handrailing as well as masking jumps in
handrail alignment (refer forward to
Figure 6.5e). In times past such work
was entirely framed in oak enriched
with carvings and statuary as at Hatfield
House (Figure 6.4c), perhaps the finest
Jacobean staircase in England. More
comely versions exist in the Inns of
Court and at the former offices of the
Architectural Press in Queen Anne's
Gate (Figure 6.4a).

6.2 Curved framing

The continuous line of curved stairs is
more enticing than the interruptions
caused by newels. Timber framing in
the form of laminated strings assisted
by a wrought-iron flitch plate date back
to the eighteenth century (see Figure
6.1c), though carpenters often propped
their work with a slender iron column
as extra security. Otto Salvisberg at
Roche Chemicals, Welwyn Garden City,

Typical options from suppliers of standard stairs
including newels and balustrade kits

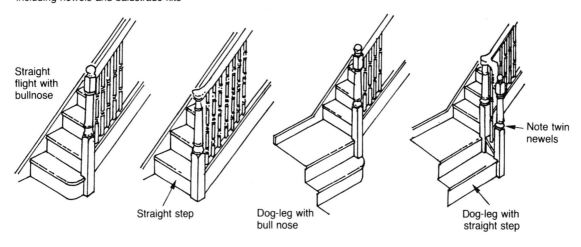

Straight
flight with
bullnose

Straight step

Dog-leg with
bull nose

Dog-leg with
straight step

Note twin
newels

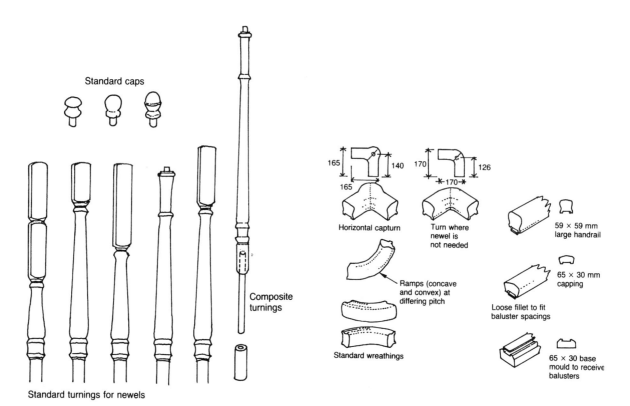

Standard caps

Composite
turnings

Standard turnings for newels

165   140   170   126

165   170

Horizontal capturn

Turn where
newel is
not needed

59 × 59 mm
large handrail

65 × 30 mm
capping

Loose fillet to fit
baluster spacings

Ramps (concave
and convex) at
differing pitch

Standard wreathings

65 × 30 base
mould to receive
balusters

Figure 6.3 Typical page from manufacturer's catalogue (by kind permission of Richard Burbidge & Son Ltd)

Figure 6.4a Historic examples: Stairs in Queen Anne's Gate, London, 1704, from Cruikshank, D. and Burton, N., Life in the Georgian City, *Viking, 1990*

put in a chromium-plated tube to camouflage his belt and braces attitude to curved strings rising 3 800 mm (Figure 6.5*a*).

The construction resembles the open tread stair except that the strings are made from glued ply or blocks (like laminboard) with face veneers and lippings. The integral strength comes from

the tread acting with the inner and outer strings (Figure 6.5*b*). An alternative strategy is to use a central post, either solid or laminated, as a drum to carry the tapered end to each tread (Figure 6.5*c*). A more elegant solution found in Central Europe is to carve a curved newel into a hollow half cylinder. This shape fulfils the role of a newel in supporting treads,

Figure 6.4b Historic examples: Replacement stair, Morton House, Highgate, London, 1990 (Julian Harrap)

Figure 6.4c Historic examples: Hatfield House Stairs, 1620

as well as the inner strings and handrail (Figure 6.5*d*), without destroying the line of the balustrade. (Compare with Figure 6.5*e* for a traditional solution.) Carpenters' manuals from the eighteenth and nineteenth century are worth studying. Figure 6.5*f* reveals the geometry of oval stairs similar to the elegance in Figure 6.1*c*.

6.3 Non-traditional framing

Box construction with plywood enables winders to be constructed without relying on traditional wreathed strings, the general arrangement is given in Figure 6.6*a*. The plywood is fixed to the envel-

ope walls behind a dog-leg stair whilst the boxed newel is set up for framing the winders; the remaining straight flights can be assembled from open treads or cased in with tread and riser as required.

Wooden treads can be suspended from the trimming timbers of the floor above (refer forward to Figure 7.6*b*). Here the suspenders support the string, but this can also be adapted to support individual treads on short battens, as designed by Walter Segal for self-build clients (Figure 6.6*b*). If hangers are placed at the edge of nosings, an intermediate baluster has to be provided to reduce the space between balusters to the maximum of 100 mm.

Figure 6.5a Curved framing: Curved flight, Roche Chemicals, Welwyn Garden City, 1938, Architect: Otto Salvisberg (from Schuster, F., Treppen, Homan Verlag, 1949)

6.4 Tread detailing

The traditional 'cased in' stair has a nosing edge dictated by the housing joint of the riser (Figure 6.7a). A further complication occurs with cut strings where the nosing profile is reflected as a trimming feature to each exposed step (Figure 6.7b). Carpet finishing in such circumstances implies painted margins and the unsightly look of the selvedge behind the balusters. Straight strings avoid these complications (Figure 6.7c).

A complaint about open timber tread stairs is their noisiness in use and the difficulties that arise in coverings. Replaceable nosings will permit a range of finishings to be applied, the treads being considered as individual trays (refer back to Figure 6.2c).

6.5 Balustrade detailing

British Building Regulations are set forth in Chapter 10, not to mention the British Building Inspectors' 100 mm spherical ball. Patterns based upon 100 mm intervals may pall and it is worth considering varied spacing to improve the scale or to vary the girth of the baluster (Figure 6.8a). In practical terms it is an easy matter to construct a vertical rod balustrade in timber provided adequate purchase exists in

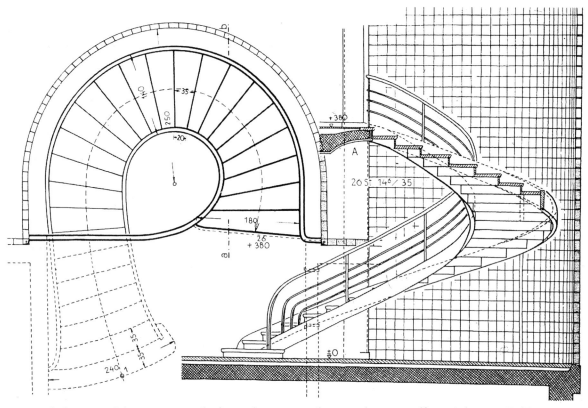

Figure 6.5b Curved framing: Detail of circular stair with central support (from Schuster, F., Treppen, *Homan Verlag, 1949)*

the string and landing nosing (refer back to Figure 6.2*d*). For tread ends in cut strings refer to Figure 6.7*b*. Horizontal rail designs are simpler to frame up with newel posts (Figure 6.8*b*) and make a stout barrier if threaded through with tubular steel, but horizontal rails can be dangerous where children may try to climb them. In the same vein, the inclusion of metal rod verticals within a timber balustrade will considerably stiffen the construction. Another age-old device, from observing stairs in Georgian houses, is the discreet metal bracket that pins the underside of the handrail to a fixing on the apron lining (Figure 6.8*c*). Mesh and sheet panels usually require metal framing to give adequate strength where the choice rests with proprietary systems (Figure 6.8*f*).

Problems now exist with historic buildings open to the public where the balusters are spaced too far apart. One solution is to place a glass or perspex panel against the balusters. At Eltham Palace, English Heritage have provided a knotted cord protection which adds a decorative feature to the otherwise unsafe stair (Figure 6.8*g*).

6.6 Handrailing

The traditional kit stairs mentioned in Section 6.1 (Figure 6.3) have the attraction that standardized wreathings and terminal blocks are available, even though the shapes have the coarseness of Edwardiana. Equal economy can ensue if

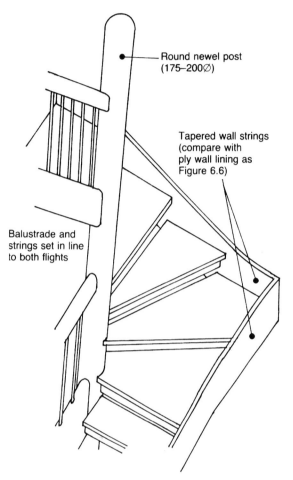

Round newel post
(175–200∅)

Tapered wall strings
(compare with
ply wall lining as
Figure 6.6)

Balustrade and
strings set in line
to both flights

*Figure 6.5c Curved framing: Detail of winders
with post support*

*Figure 6.5d Curved framing: Curved newel to
support strings and handrail, Wood House,
Shipbourne, 1938, Architects: Gropius and Fry*

standard mopstick handrails are used without wreathing. Once turned work is needed then the services of specialists will be required to fabricate wreathed work at stairwells and for terminal blocks etc. The handrailing connections are made by special bolts (Figure 6.8*d* and *e*); various attempts have been tried to market a universal timber handrailing that will solve all circular work. Metal fabricators have come nearest to this ideal and would appear to hold the key to composite designs where timber stairs are combined with glass, mesh or sheet balustrading.

The comfortable feel of timber to the touch should not be forgotten. Handrails are shaped to be grasped, the simple mopstick (45 mm diameter) or oval (64 mm × 40 mm) are immensely comfortable and much superior to the brutalist bulks favoured in the 1960s (Figure 6.8*h*). Complex shapes were developed by Aalto to provide anthropomorphic forms to fit the hand (Figure 6.8*i*) but the cost of wreathing is formidable.

6.7 Trimming detail

Timber stairs should preferably be fitted after plastering in order to protect the

Figure 6.5e Curved framing: Traditional newel post

woodwork and to provide a movement joint between the wall string and the finished surfaces (Figures 6.9a and 6.9b). The fixing of wooden flights is a matter of propping against trimmers with a housing joint, the base can easily be secured by dowel or coach bolt. A timber apron lining surmounted by a capping will provide a suitable edge trim to wooden floors. The advantage of a wide capping is the better fit that can be made for balustrade fixing, apart from the opportunity to match the profile of the treads at the well location (refer to Figure 6.2c). Landings will need trimming to support wide treads and winders as Figure 6.9c).

6.8 Tactile quality

The tactile quality of timber can be sensed from the lead-in pictures. It is a matter of form and texture which gives as much pleasure to the maker as to the user. The early twelfth-century primitive steps are solid in construction and contrast with the elegant form of the Miraculous Stairs (Figure 6.1d), apparently built without nails by a travelling carpenter who came and went without being paid, another sample of devoted work. The nuns at the little church called Our Lady of Light Chapel, Sante Fe, still whisper under their breath that the itinerant stairmaker was called Joseph.

There is little doubt that the United States was provided with a great range of inspired work by Europeans emigrés. The Gamble House, Pasadena (according to the guide book), owes the finishing work entirely to European skill. The aesthetic direction of the designers Greene and Greene may be Japan (Figure 6.1b) but the enveloping skill that assembled the handcarved stair encapsulates the joy of working in wood that is found in alpine chalets. Modern techniques with laminboard and ply can be equally inspiring as portrayed in a spiral stair designed by Luisa Parisi (Figure 6.10a), an example of lineal sculpture in space and equal to the invention of Victor Horta (Figure 6.10b). The geometry of propped and suspended construction has intrigued many designers. An interesting concept is featured in the concluding illustration (Figure 6.11) which combines both features within one staircase. The traditional cased stair was removed in a cottage conversion and new framing made in the form of shelf construction.

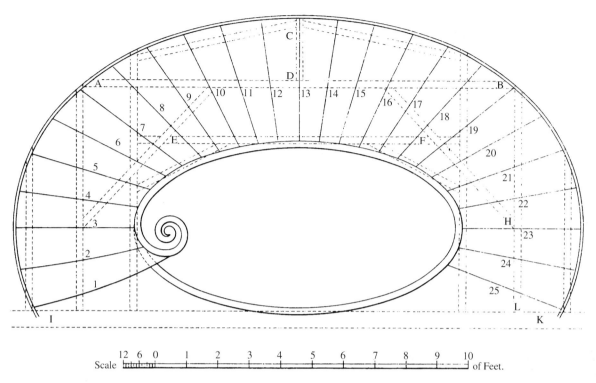

Figure 6.5f Curved framing: Georgian elliptical stairs (from Newland, J., The Carpenter's Assistant, *Studio Editions, 1990)*

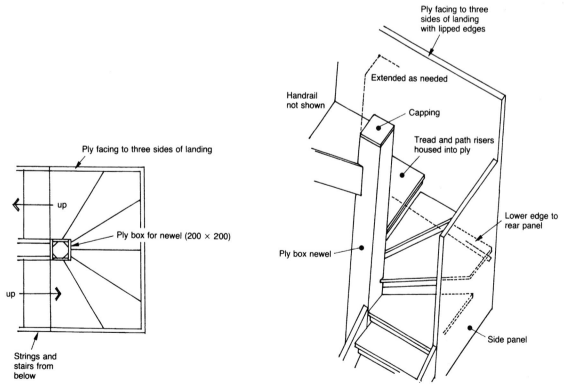

Figure 6.6a Sketch details for plywood framing

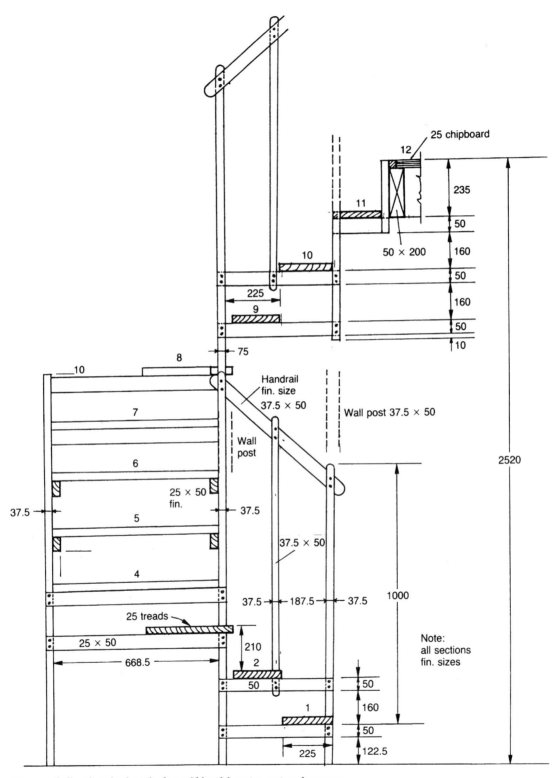

Figure 6.6b Sketch details for self-build stairs using hangers

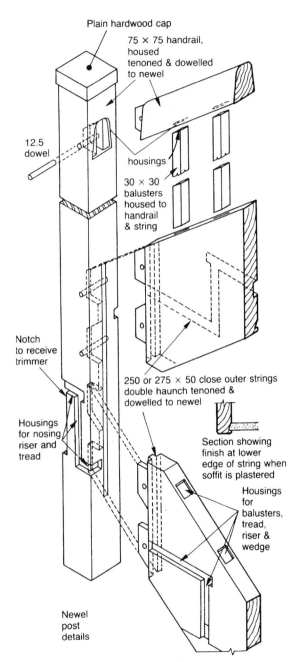

Plain hardwood cap

75 × 75 handrail, housed tenoned & dowelled to newel

12.5 dowel

housings

30 × 30 balusters housed to handrail & string

Notch to receive trimmer

Housings for nosing riser and tread

250 or 275 × 50 close outer strings double haunch tenoned & dowelled to newel

Section showing finish at lower edge of string when soffit is plastered

Housings for balusters, tread, riser & wedge

Newel post details

Figure 6.7a Principles of cased construction: Traditional detailing

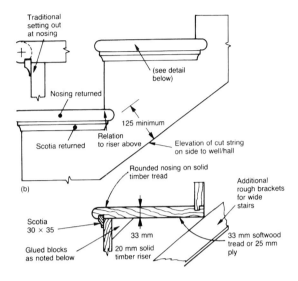

Traditional setting out at nosing

Nosing returned

Scotia returned

Relation to riser above

(see detail below)

125 minimum

Elevation of cut string on side to well/hall

(b)

Rounded nosing on solid timber tread

Additional rough brackets for wide stairs

Scotia 30 × 35

33 mm

33 mm softwood tread or 25 mm ply

Glued blocks as noted below

20 mm solid timber riser

Figure 6.7b Principles of cased construction: Cut tread nosing

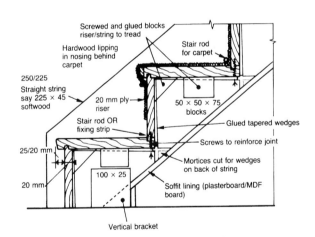

Screwed and glued blocks riser/string to tread

Hardwood lipping in nosing behind carpet

Stair rod for carpet

250/225 Straight string say 225 × 45 softwood

20 mm ply riser

50 × 50 × 75 blocks

Glued tapered wedges

Stair rod OR fixing strip

Screws to reinforce joint

25/20 mm

Mortices cut for wedges on back of string

20 mm

100 × 25

Soffit lining (plasterboard/MDF board)

Vertical bracket

Figure 6.7c Principles of cased construction: Nosings for straight string stairs

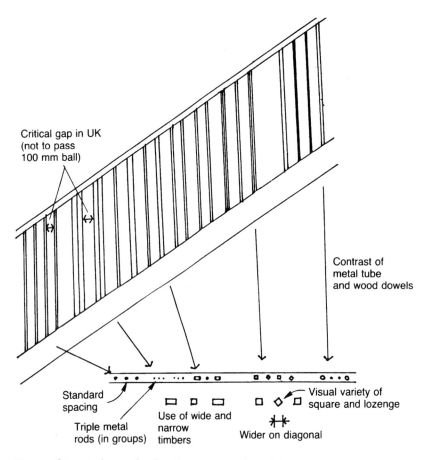

Figure 6.8a Balustrade detailing: Vertical and horizontal rail balustrade

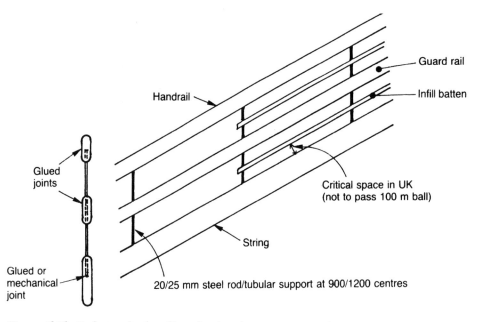

Figure 6.8b Balustrade detailing: Steel rod supports to rails

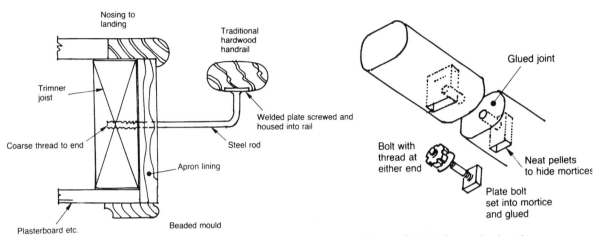

Figure 6.8c Balustrade detailing: Discrete handrail bracket

Figure 6.8e Balustrade detailing: Handrail bolts

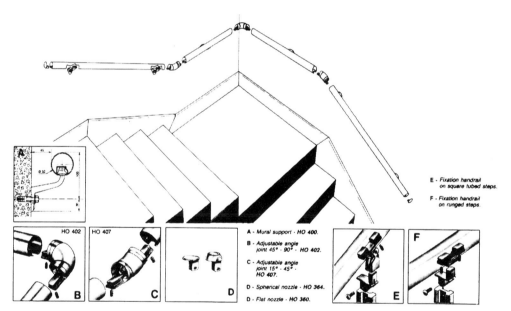

Figure 6.8d Balustrade detailing: Proprietary systems for handrailing (reprinted by kind permission of Kensington Traders Ltd)

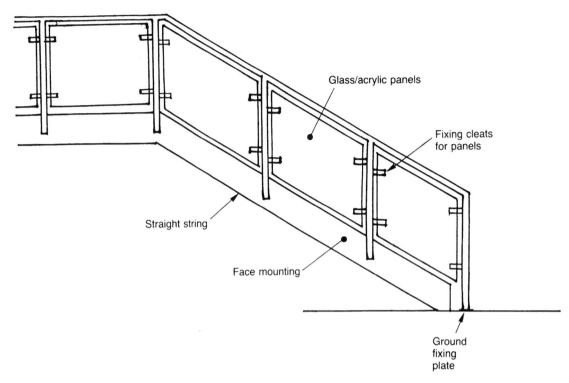

Figure 6.8f Balustrade detailing: Universal balustrading. Hewi system using metal tubular sections and panels

Figure 6.8g Balustrade detailing: Eltham Palace. Details of remedial protection

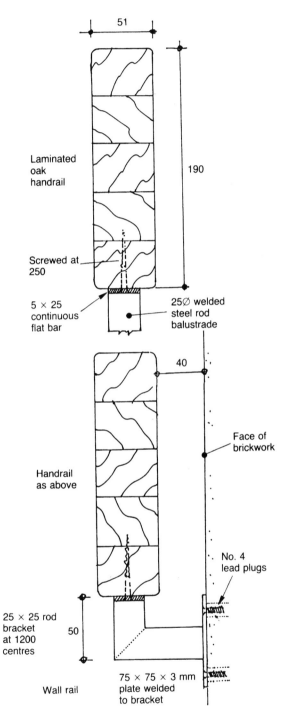

51

190

Laminated
oak
handrail

Screwed at
250

5 × 25
continuous
flat bar

25⌀ welded
steel rod
balustrade

40

Face of
brickwork

Handrail
as above

No. 4
lead plugs

25 × 25 rod
bracket
at 1200
centres

50

75 × 75 × 3 mm
plate welded
to bracket

Wall rail

Figure 6.8b Balustrade detailing: Brutalist profile

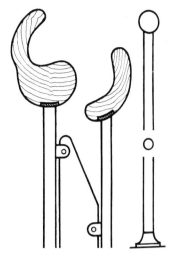

*Figure 6.8i Balustrade detailing: Aalto's
anthropomorphic handrails (from Schuster, F.,*
Treppen, *Homan Verlag, 1949)*

The lowermost element is a bookcase
with stair treads to the back, whilst the
suspended upper flight is made from
balustrade boards extended downward
to support the last few treads.

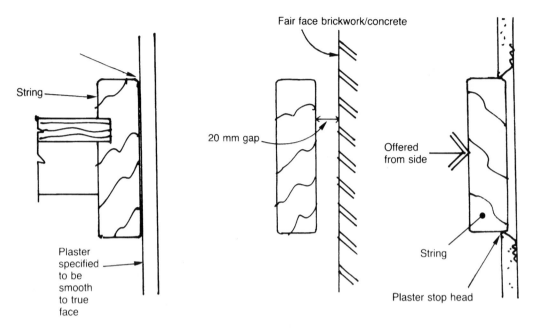

Fair face brickwork/concrete

String

20 mm gap

Offered
from side

String

Plaster
specified
to be
smooth
to true
face

Plaster stop head

Figure 6.9a Trimming details:String and plaster movement joint

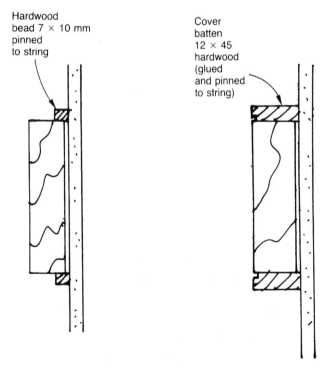

Hardwood
bead 7 × 10 mm
pinned
to string

Cover
batten
12 × 45
hardwood
(glued
and pinned
to string)

Figure 6.9b Trimming details: Covermoulds

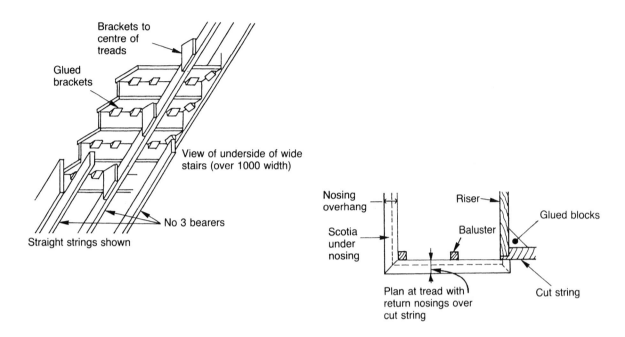

Brackets to
centre of
treads

Glued
brackets

View of underside of wide
stairs (over 1000 width)

No 3 bearers

Straight strings shown

Nosing
overhang

Scotia
under
nosing

Riser

Baluster

Glued blocks

Cut string

Plan at tread with
return nosings over
cut string

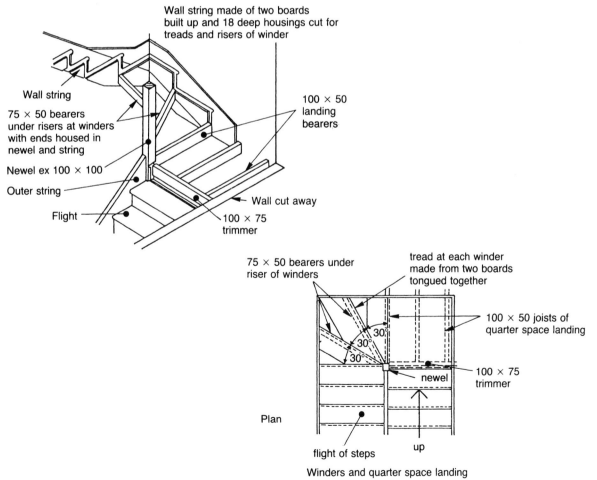

Wall string made of two boards
built up and 18 deep housings cut for
treads and risers of winder

Wall string

75 × 50 bearers
under risers at winders
with ends housed in
newel and string

Newel ex 100 × 100

Outer string

Flight

100 × 50
landing
bearers

Wall cut away

100 × 75
trimmer

75 × 50 bearers under
riser of winders

tread at each winder
made from two boards
tongued together

30°
30°
30°

100 × 50 joists of
quarter space landing

newel

100 × 75
trimmer

Plan

flight of steps

up

Winders and quarter space landing

Figure 6.9c Trimming at landings and winders (from Barry, R., The Construction of Buildings, *Vol. 2,*
Blackwell Scientific Publications, 1992)

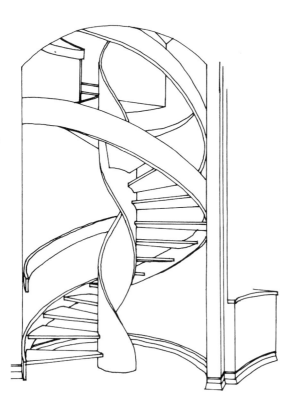

Figure 6.10a Lineal sculpture in space: Plywood stairs by Luisa Parisi (from Aloi, G., Scale, Ulrico Hoepli, 1973)

Figure 6.10b Victor Horta's handrail and newel post at his house in Brussels

Figure 6.11 Stair framing considered as furniture at Walmer 1975, Architect: John Bruckland

References

1   Carpenters' manuals – *The Carpenter's Assistant* by James Newlands (in fascimile by Studio Editions, 1990). *The British Architect or the Builders Treasury of Staircases* by Swan (1775).

2   Standard suppliers' catalogues – Domestic staircases are very much part of the 'bricolage' which governs house building on both sides of the Atlantic. In the UK the leading components' suppliers for stairs are Richard Burbidge & Son Ltd, Botrea Stairs (Saxondell Ltd) and John Carr Joinery Sales Ltd, each of which produce almost identical catalogues.

7 Detailed construction: iron, steel and other metals

7.1 Ladders and ladder steps

Cast- and wrought-iron work in ladders and stairs has a tradition that stems from the Industrial Revolution (Figures 7.1*a* and 7.1*b*). Another source is the spider's web of steps that straddle the Eiffel Tower. The lattice girders were designed as ladders to enable the repainting to be carried out without cradles or scaffold.

The addition of lightly framed steel stairs and handrailing can be less intrusive than masonry construction when making ruins accessible for tourists. At Rochester Castle, John Winter was asked to insert floors and add a roof to the open shell of the ruined tower. He was also asked to construct a staircase in such a position that the public could enter the castle

Figure 7.1b Copper coated wrought-iron stairs, Stock Exchange Building, Chicago, 1893–4, Architects: Adler and Sullivan

Figure 7.1a Cast-iron sectional spiral stairs, Palm House, Kew Gardens, London, 1844–8, Designers: Turner and Burton

through the original doorway. It is not known how the original stairs or roof were constructed, so it was decided to make these modern structures, but to keep them discreet so that the famous views of the castle were not affected. The staircase is a simple structure of steel bars and plate with oak treads. It is

Figure 7.1c Addition of external steel stairs to Rochester Castle for visitor access, 1990, John Winter (courtesy of John Donat)

finely detailed and makes a neat foil against the old stonework (Figure 7.1*c*).

7.2 Fire escape stairs

These are a more familiar pattern and where iron and steel are still employed in fabrication. The traditional construction relies on steel strings (formerly plate) with angle supports for cast-iron fretted treads, often strengthened by castings for the risers (Figure 7.2*a*). In the USA the external fire stairs are part of the vernacular architecture in the inner city (Figure 7.2*b*). They are sometimes considered as

an integral element of the façade (as on Hallidie Building, Figure 3.22), instead of becoming the visual accident that is commonplace. The American approach to fire escapes is more dramatic owing to the hinged security steps for the lowermost flights.

Fire escape construction is generally a mundane affair, with column supports for framed landings and dog-leg flights spanning as infill (Figures 7.2*c* and 7.2*d*). Detailing with structural sections requires skill to overcome clumsiness at connecting points. Salvisberg's detailing is exemplary in the instance chosen where members are splayed or cut to ensure a neat geometry. The construction

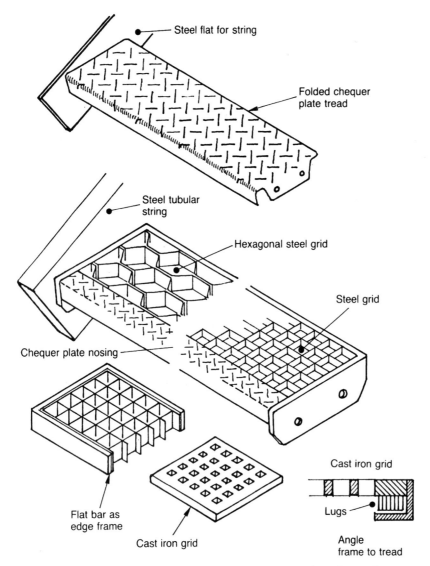

Figure 7.2a Ladders and fire escape stairs: Details of traditional cast-iron and steel treads and risers

is conventional using 12.5 mm plate for strings and 105 mm × 105 mm tees with tubular rails (Figure 7.2e). Arne Jacobsen has solved the problem of an obtrusive external stair by encasing in a cylinder of fire resisting glazing (Figure 7.2f).

Security can be effected by caging the fire stairs with exit gates at ground level (Figure 7.2g). The requirements of fire officers will include emergency lighting, fire resisting glazing to windows within a prescribed distance and weather protection unless heated treads are provided.

In the UK external steel escape stairs are subject to licence and therefore regular inspections are needed to check on condition and repairs. Galvanizing the iron and steel components of the structure will prolong their life, delaying the paint treatment by ten or so years will increase the bond between paint and the zinc-coated surfaces.

Figure 7.2b Vernacular escape stairs in USA

Figure 7.2c Typical tubular framing to support landings of dog-leg stairs, offices at Stockley Park, 1989, Architects: Arup Associates

In the Centre Pompidou, Paris, the principal movement areas are totally contained within the building envelope, whilst emergency routes are largely external. Space is generally the problem but at Stockley Park there is an elegant solution for secondary external stairs (Figure 7.2*b*) which can be bolted onto façades as required.

7.3 Standard internal stairs

Fabrication methods devised for external stairs can be applied to internal stairs as with the Technical High School, Basle (Figure 7.2*d*). Open grid and chequer plate stairs are also used for industrial work. A higher standard of finish can be accommodated within metal trays or else laid on sheet steel formwork. The generic term is a 'folded sheet stair' welded to plate or tubular strings. It is this type of industrialized steel stair that is widely adopted in commercial buildings, particularly with steel frame construction. The advantages are linked to 'fast track' methods where the skeletal frame and stairs are erected in advance of floors and envelope walls, the folded sheet stair, even as formwork, provides access for the buildings without the need for scaffolding towers. The pattern depends upon the finishes to be applied ultimately on site; Figures 7.3*a–c* depict the selection offered by fabricators and the range of finishes which can be achieved.

Individual trays can be fitted just before handover to save wear and tear in construction and can be used with stairs framed in timber or pre-cast concrete (Figure 7.3*d*).

Figure 7.2d Typical RSJ framing: escape stairs, Technical High School, Basle, 1931, Architect: Otto Salvisberg (from Schuster, F., Treppen, Hoffman Verlag, *1949)*

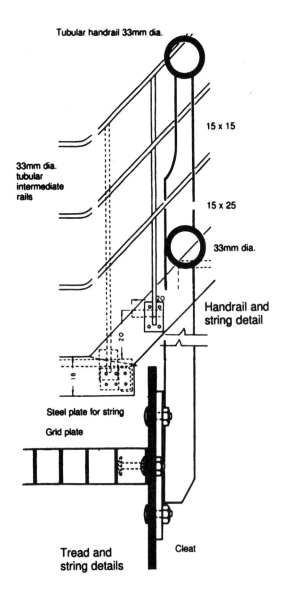

7.4 Spiral stairs

Steel spiral stairs are also the subject of industrial production and supplied as a package of parts. A typical assembly comprises a centre column and base plate, over which the cantilever treads or landings are sleeved, with cotter pins to secure each component in place (Figure 7.4a). The handrail and rod balustrade stiffen the outside edge of the spiral. Welding the balustrade to guard rails can provide a structural lattice which acts as a supporting member; another method is to design a trussed balustrade (Figure 7.4b). The tread details follow the principles of 'steel trays' already discussed, with var-

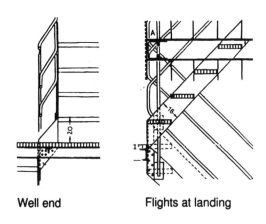

Figure 7.2e Balustrade details

Figure 7.2f Minimal escape stairs with glass enclosure, 'Novo' factory, Copenhagen, 1961, Architect: Arne Jacobsen (Danish regulations permit spiral escapes)

Figure 7.2g Security enclosure to stairs (courtesy of Weland Grating (UK) Ltd)

ious materials acting as a facing or infilling. Designer spirals have reached beyond the limit of common sense in France with polished aluminum castings resembling giant teaspoons that are jettied off a spinal vertebra (Figure 7.4c). Patterns of nineteenth-century engineering are still manufactured, the developments in replica casting means that historic features can be matched. The spiral stairs and balconies at the Palm House, Kew, are a case in point (Figure 7.1a), where the naturalistic forms still perfectly echo the natural plant material.

Figure 7.2h External escape stairs, Apple Computer's Facility Stockley Park, 1989, Architects: Troughton McAslan

Figure 7.3a Folded steel stairs: Providing builders access as skeletal frame is erected and then used permanently

7.5 Special stairs

Welded plate formed into hollow tubular members gives the greatest freedom in design. The possibilities with cantilevers are more rewarding than standard spirals where bolted connections may loosen. The example at Arnhem City Hall in Figure 7.5a has a flair and verve that equals the finest work by Victor Horta. The imaginative use of curved rectangular tube in handrailing recreates the sinuous

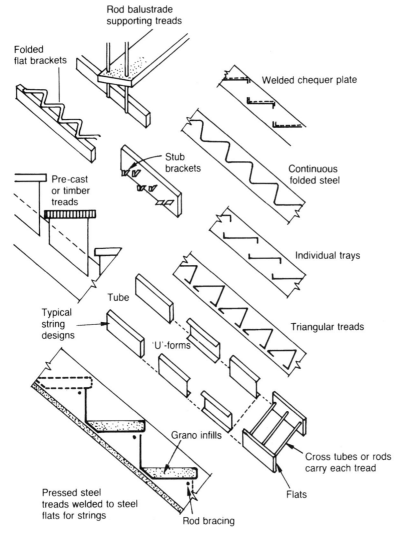

Figure 7.3b Folded steel stairs: Profiles for folded sheet stairs or treads

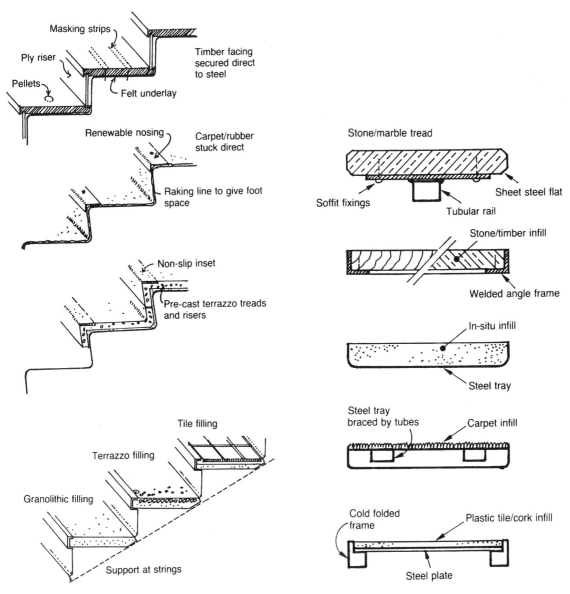

Figure 7.3c Folded steel stairs: Finishes to folded plate

Figure 7.3d Folded steel stairs: Individual tread detailing

qualities associated with metals and is employed to maximum effect where the rails terminate as newels.

Public stairs within this idiom need to have a safe balustrade, such as I. M. Pei's detail for the new entry below the Grand Louvre pyramid (given in Case Study 12.4). Curved sheets of toughened glass or acrylic (if permitted by fire codes)

have inherent strength and sufficient rigidity to perform as a balustrade if effectively clamped to the handrail and string (Figures 7.5*b* and 7.5*c*). The engineering to the Foster stairs and bridge at the Sainsbury Arts Centre, Norwich, had to be tested with the built example on site to satisfy the local authority in 1977, though the construction principles are

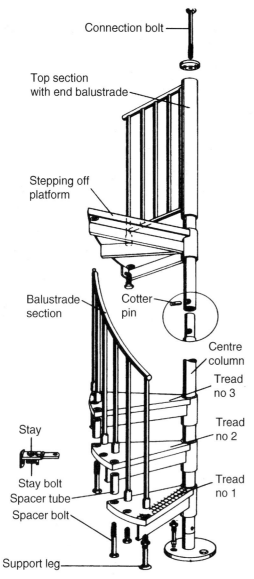

Connection bolt

Top section
with end balustrade

Stepping off
platform

Balustrade
section

Cotter
pin

Centre
column

Tread
no 3

Tread
no 2

Stay

Stay bolt
Spacer tube
Spacer bolt

Tread
no 1

Support leg

Figure 7.4a Spiral stairs: Typical assembly of centre column with cantilever treads and landings (with kind permission of Weland Grating (UK) Ltd)

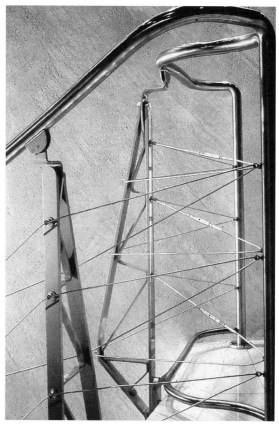

Figure 7.4b Spiral stairs: Lattice frame to balustrading: detail of trussed balustrade to curving stairs at Legends night club, London, 1987, Architect: Eva Jiricna, Engineers: Dewhurst MacFarlane

now fully accepted and marketed as standard balustrades.[1]

Glass and metal can also be combined in treads and risers. Le Corbusier used 'Nevada' lenscrete to diffuse natural lighting to the stairwell in the Maison Clarté apartment building in Geneva (Figure 7.5*d*). The artificial lighting was arranged through a suspended conduit in the well

serviced by naked light bulbs – replacement of the bulbs was effected by sliding the light fixture along its overhead track at the top floor and then walking down to each landing to change the bulb. The slender quality of steel profiles can reduce the impact of pre-cast concrete or timber which may be selected for treads. Ladder trusses with horizontal steel trellises will carry 'plank' treads, the upper line of the trusses forming a handrail. This motif was used frequently by Marcel Breuer for external stairs to reduce the impact or shadow from the construction interfering with the fenestration (Figure 7.5*e*).

Figure 7.4c Spiral stairs: Designer spirals beyond the limit of common sense

Figure 7.5a Special stairs: Welded plate to form hollow profiles for newel and for cantilever treads: accommodation stairs at City Hall, Arnhem, General view

7.6 Suspended stairs

Suspended stairs have already been alluded to in Asplund's Courthouse (referring back to Figures 2.7*a* and 2.7*b*). The concept usually relies on individual rod suspension or else a structural balustrade which suspends the treads along the bottom chord (Figures 7.6*a–d*).

A lattice structure can be made by connecting handrail, balustrade and undercarriage brackets; various patents exist that apply to both curving and straight flights. Welding balusters either as a horizontal frame (the hallmark of Marcel Breuer's designs) or as a trellis or vertical pattern are other alternatives. Suspension wires can be used to secure wooden treads, one of the most minimal solutions being devised by Peter Moro at the former Hille showroom. The interior is now destroyed but is recalled to demonstrate the thesis 'least is most' with this example of slender detail (Figure 7.6*d*). The most interesting combination of trussed suspensions has been developed by Eva Jiricna and her engineer consultants. One of the best crafted stairs is the triple flight incorporated into the Joseph Store, Sloane Street (Figure 7.7*a–c*). The sculptural effect of this stair is closer to furniture with the engineering honed to the absolute minimum. The lightness of this eye-

Figure 7.5b Spiral stairs, Sainsbury Arts Centre, Anglia University, 1977, Architect: Foster and Partners

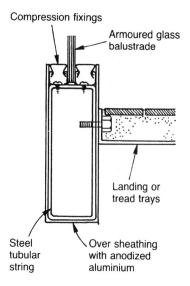

Figure 7.5c Construction detail of balustrade and string, spiral stairs, Sainsbury Arts Centre

Figure 7.5d 'Nevada' glass used in treads to Maison Clarté, Geneva, 1932, Architect: Le Corbusier

Figure 7.5e Ladder trusses carrying treads, Einstein Village, Princeton, USA, Architect: Marcel Breuer

Figure 7.6a Suspended stairs: Patented balustrade brackets (by kind permission of Ictoni Spiral Staircase Systems)

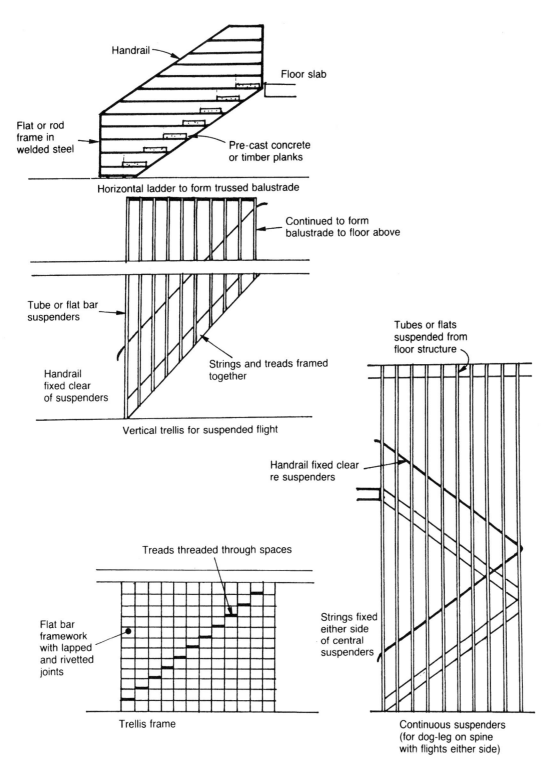

Handrail

Floor slab

Flat or rod frame in welded steel

Pre-cast concrete or timber planks

Horizontal ladder to form trussed balustrade

Continued to form balustrade to floor above

Tube or flat bar suspenders

Handrail fixed clear of suspenders

Strings and treads framed together

Vertical trellis for suspended flight

Tubes or flats suspended from floor structure

Handrail fixed clear re suspenders

Treads threaded through spaces

Flat bar framework with lapped and rivetted joints

Strings fixed either side of central suspenders

Trellis frame

Continuous suspenders (for dog-leg on spine with flights either side)

Figure 7.6b Suspended stairs: Balustrade trusses

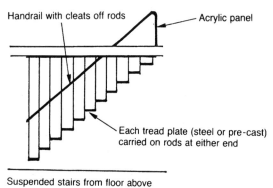

Suspension rods

Handrail

Fixed to side of suspenders

Acrylic panel
with distance
brackets

Tubular
suspenders

Folded steel
plate stairs

Vertical suspenders
to carry steel
plate stairs

Head plate

Timber handrails
and strings to open
stairs

Cables to
infill between
suspenders

Panels for
handrail and
balustrade
with string
face fixed
to suspenders

Anchor
plates

Vertical suspenders
threaded through handrails
and strings

Handrail with cleats off rods

Acrylic panel

Each tread plate (steel or pre-cast)
carried on rods at either end

Suspended stairs from floor above

Figure 7.6c Suspended stairs

Figure 7.6d Suspended stairs: Cable suspension, former Hille Showroom, London, 1963, Architect: Peter Moro

Figure 7.7b General view (see also Figure 3.19b)

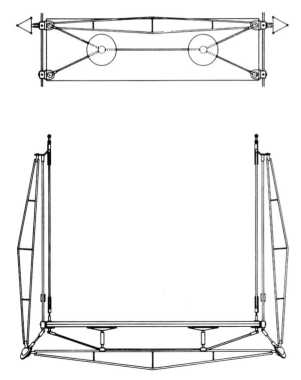

Figure 7.7a Suspended stairs, Joseph Store, Sloane Street, London, 1989, Architect: Eva Jiricna, Engineer: Matthew Wells of Barton and Wells: Details: plan and section through typical tread

Figure 7.7c Detail of structure

catcher is enhanced by glass treads and balustrading whilst the structure itself is an assembly of stretched cables, stainless rods and connectors providing a spider's web of supporting members. The art of constructing stairs when this level of skill is required is a combination of architectural and engineering input, hence the multiple credits to Eva Jiricna and Matthew Wells, now a partner with the consulting engineers Barton and Wells.

7.7 Metal balustrading

The choice of bronze or steel for balustrading is dictated by the engineering. Problems with the proven strength of bronze imply that bronze, like aluminium, is often utilized as a sacrificial surface over steel cores in structuring balustrades. The constructional restraints are governed in the UK by Codes of Practice[2] and are concerned with lateral strength and fixings. This is a separate issue to that raised by the Jiricna–Wells suspended stairs where the total ensemble of balustrading and stair framing have to be assessed as structural engineering.

The traditional concept can be compared to a framework infill, comprising the following elements and illustrated in Figures 7.8a–g.

- Vertical members, termed standards, provide the main support.
- Rails, termed handrails and core rails, the latter making a sub-frame (if needed) for the infilling members.
- Balustrades, formed with bars, mesh or sheet materials.
- Connections, welding, set screws, sleeves and cleated brackets.

The assembled framework is connected together in panels by set screws and on-site welding. The supporting strings can be timber, steel (plate or tubular) or reinforced concrete (either *in situ* or pre-cast) (Figure 7.8g).

The geometry of the assembly is critical to the overall stability: long runs to landings and straight flights will need heavier standards or stays. Shorter flights with dog-leg or triple-turn layouts provide sufficient return lengths to stiffen the framing. Circular balustrading is also stiffer than straight runs.

Base fixings are another factor; direct vertical fixings have less torque than side-mounted standards. The advantage of the former stems from the face-to-face bolting that can be obtained from base plates to the stair or landing structure, with loading in line with the standards. The actual connections vary with the stairs: refer to Figure 7.8 for a range of alternative details.

Side fixings into the edge of treads or landings save space since Building Codes in the UK and the USA permit the required stair width to be measured to the edge of the handrail. The actual girth of tread is therefore minimal as compared with base-mounted balustrades which can add 75 mm to the width of stair or landing construction at balustrade locations. Side fixings do not necessarily save space since the well size has to be sufficient to accommodate the 'L'-shaped standards apart from adequate dimensions if wreathings are employed. Balustrades set clear of tread and landing surfaces have the crucial advantage that floor coverings are not perforated which makes maintenance and replacement an easier proposition.

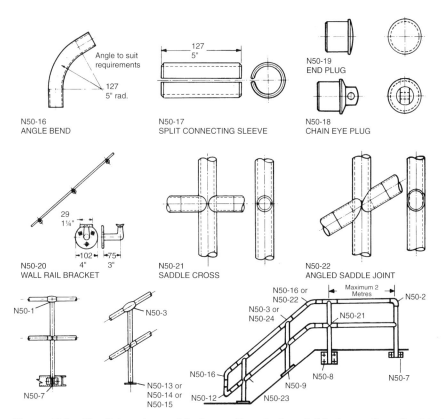

Figure 7.8a Traditional metal balustrading: Industrial balustrading (by kind permission of Norton Engineering Alloys Co. Ltd)

A compromise solution is to devise a string component for both treads and landings which contains vertical fixings for the balustrading and horizontal connections to the surrounding structure. Traditional detailing involves hardwood sections (Figure 7.8g) but tubular steel sections or pre-cast concrete will serve equally well; the latter has the advantage that factory finishes such as terrazzo or tile can be applied to give a high quality setting for the balustrade. The arrangement also means that the minimal structural width can be provided for treads, etc., whilst the handrail/standard/string component occupies a zone within the well. Straight string features that project above nosing lines to stairs and landings also facilitate maintenance whereby cleaning operations do not spill dirt down into the staircase well.

The 'guarding' rules for balustrades to stairs and landings under the National Building Regulations are explained in Section 10.2 with illustrations in Figure 10.2. The worst situation occurs where multi-occupancy is planned and the designer is faced with a variety of conflicting advice under the Regulations as to the ideal height for the handrail. Aalto resolved this dilemma by running handrails in duplicate, one for the adults and one for the children.

Another sensible solution is to choose a standard height for the principal balustrade element, be it railings or walling, and then mount the handrail separately to follow the mandate of the Regulations.

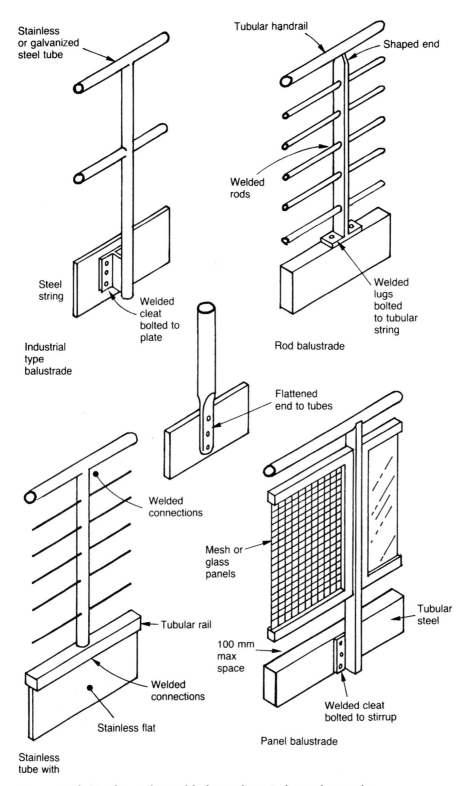

Stainless
or galvanized
steel tube

Tubular handrail

Shaped end

Welded
rods

Steel
string

Welded
cleat
bolted to
plate

Industrial
type
balustrade

Welded
lugs
bolted
to tubular
string

Rod balustrade

Flattened
end to tubes

Welded
connections

Mesh or
glass
panels

Tubular rail

Tubular
steel

100 mm
max
space

Welded
connections

Welded cleat
bolted to stirrup

Stainless flat

Panel balustrade

Stainless
tube with

Figure 7.8b Traditional metal balustrading: Balustrade panels

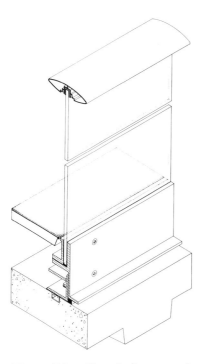

Figure 7.8c Glass & sheet panels, designed by Foster and Partners

Figure 7.8e Traditional metal balustrading: Horizontal rail (by kind permission of Aidrail Ltd)

Figure 7.8d Traditional metal balustrading: Mesh panels (by kind permission of Aidrail Ltd)

In this method the geometry of the spandrel treatment (perforate or solid) can at least match the stair geometry.

Aluminum or galvanized steel industrial guard railing is another 'off-the-peg' balustrading that is effective in certain categories of work – safety barriers for maintenance stairs and accessways, even external works. The Meccano-like components comprise universal sockets and tubes held together by inset screws. The appearance with 'arthritic' joints may not be to everyone's taste; mesh panels will need to be fitted where children are at risk.

A non-traditional concept is to place the balustrade assembly as a vertical infilling to a minimal stairwell. The panels are supported by newel posts and the handrailing bracketed to provide a continuous hand-

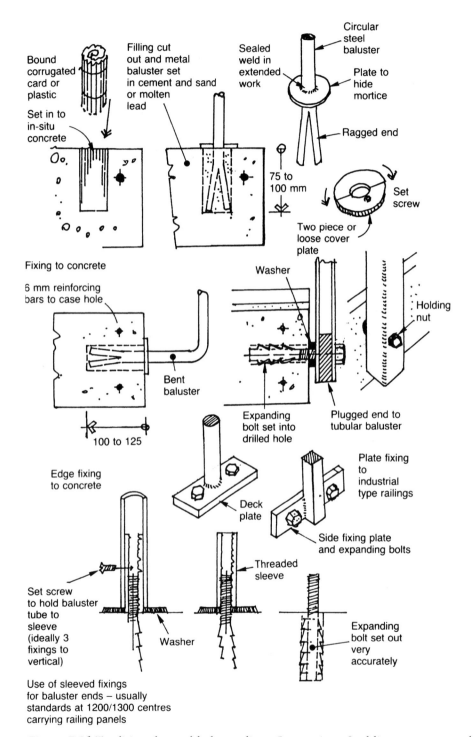

Bound corrugated card or plastic

Set in to in-situ concrete

Filling cut out and metal baluster set in cement and sand or molten lead

Sealed weld in extended work

Circular steel baluster

Plate to hide mortice

Ragged end

75 to 100 mm

Set screw

Two piece or loose cover plate

Fixing to concrete

6 mm reinforcing bars to case hole

Washer

Holding nut

Bent baluster

Expanding bolt set into drilled hole

Plugged end to tubular baluster

100 to 125

Edge fixing to concrete

Deck plate

Plate fixing to industrial type railings

Side fixing plate and expanding bolts

Set screw to hold baluster tube to sleeve (ideally 3 fixings to vertical)

Washer

Threaded sleeve

Expanding bolt set out very accurately

Use of sleeved fixings for baluster ends – usually standards at 1200/1300 centres carrying railing panels

Figure 7.8f Traditional metal balustrading: Connections (welding, set screws, sleeves & cleated brackets)

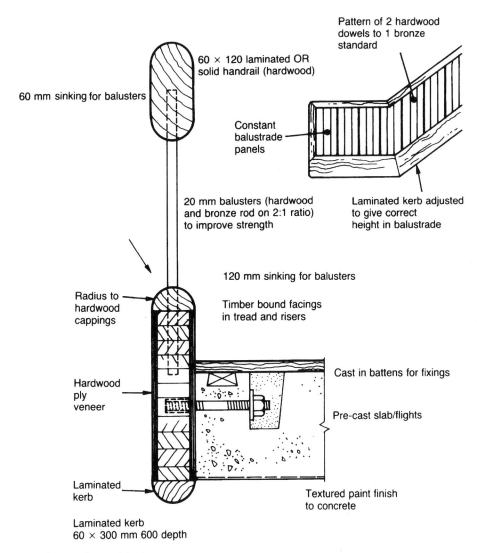

60 mm sinking for balusters

60 × 120 laminated OR solid handrail (hardwood)

Pattern of 2 hardwood dowels to 1 bronze standard

Constant balustrade panels

20 mm balusters (hardwood and bronze rod on 2:1 ratio) to improve strength

Laminated kerb adjusted to give correct height in balustrade

120 mm sinking for balusters

Radius to hardwood cappings

Timber bound facings in tread and risers

Cast in battens for fixings

Hardwood ply veneer

Pre-cast slab/flights

Laminated kerb

Textured paint finish to concrete

Laminated kerb
60 × 300 mm 600 depth

Figure 7.8g Traditional metal balustrading: String to balustrade details (timber, steel, concrete)

hold as Figure 8.5*f*. Stretched cable balustrades are another novel adaptation of marine detailing borrowed for buildings.

The rhythmic variation of metal balusters is perhaps the most memorable image (variations are given in Figures 7.9*a–d*).

Figure 7.9a Unusual construction: Wrought iron loops, John Soane Museum, London, 1790

Figure 7.9b Unusual construction: Brass frame, with handrail, enamelled standards, wires as infill and capping to string, Aarhus City Hall, 1943, Architect: Arne Jacobsen

Figure 7.9c Unusual construction: Trussed balustrade with steel handrail, verticals and folded steel treads, Havas Conseil, Paris, 1960s

Figure 7.9d Rhythmic decoration at Kedleston Stairs, 1790s, Architect: Robert Adam

References

1 Standard glass/acrylic assemblies – there are a number of handrailing specialists who fabricate standard assemblies which combine steel tubular rails with glass/acrylic. Typical products supplied in the UK are 'Hewi' (metal and glass) by Hewi (UK) Ltd; 'Neaco and Nearail' (metal and glass) by Norton Engineering Alloys Ltd and 'Horizal' (metal system) by Kensington Traders Ltd.

2 Codes of Practice – refer to BS Code 6180 (1982) for strengths required, namely sufficient to resist a horizontal force for private or common stairs and 0.74 kN for the remaining categories of stairs under UK Regulations.

8 Concrete stairs

8.1 Early forms

The earliest forms of concrete stairs are Roman where concrete was placed over brick vaulting to support ramps or steps such as in the construction of the Colosseum (Figure 8.1*a*). The introduction of filler joist flooring in the eighteenth century, with wrought-iron beams infilled by brick arches, was adapted to staircases cantilevered off masonry walls (Figure 8.1*b*).

The early use of concrete in the twentieth century was found in composite forms of building. In the case of stairs, steel joists often formed the stringers to reinforced concrete infilling (Figure 8.1*c*). Nervi, one of the finest concrete engineers, designed a minimum double-spiral stair for the Florence Sports Stadium (Figure 8.1*d*). His avant-garde approach to reinforcement design is not without problems, loss of cover to the exposed main beams having led to extensive repairs.

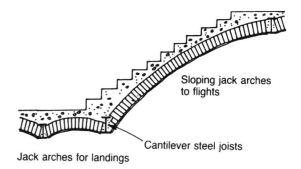

Figure 8.1b Filler joist stairs constructed with steel beams and brick vaults overlaid with rendering

Both Frank Lloyd Wright and Le Corbusier were enthusiastic exponents of reinforced concrete and realized stair designs that captured the plastic qualities of the material. The long curving ramp at the Guggenheim Museum (refer back to Figure 2.25*a* and 2.25*b*) is perhaps the most celebrated cantilevered form. Le Corbusier's designs from the heroic period (1920–30) transformed ramps and stairs into sculptured volumes that interpenetrated the floor spaces of his major buildings. The poetic geometry given to the circulation elements within the Villa Savoye (referring back to Figure 4.11) is amplified in the palatial volumes made for grand projects such as the League of Nations or the Centrosoyus Building, Moscow. The staircase structure and its relation to the plan in the Goldfinger House in Hampstead is a microcosm of the Corbusian principles, revealing the key to employing monolithic concrete to form both column and curving slab within a single stair (refer back to Figure 4.12).

Figure 8.1a Brick vaults which supported steps at the Colosseum, AD 70–82

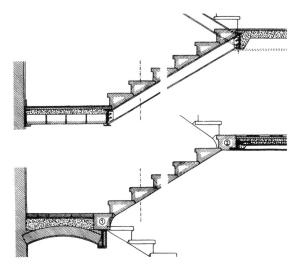

Figure 8.1c Textbook example of early reinforced concrete stairs using composite construction with steelwork

Figure 8.1d Confident use of reinforced concrete structure in stairs, Florence Stadium, 1932, Engineer: Pier Luigi Nervi

8.2 Developed forms of reinforced concrete stairs

In situ reinforced concrete has the same limitation of span to thickness as floor slabs so that single span flights are limited to about 4500 mm unless downstand spine beams or upstand balustrade beams are used. The spine beam version is usually pre-cast and implies pre-cast or metal-framed cantilever treads.

Dog-leg stairs are usually carried on cross beams at half landings or else on a thickened landing slab. Balustrade beams convert slab forms into slabs with twin upstand components which permit clear spans floor-to-floor with dramatic shapes as exemplified in the foyer to Sir Denys Lasdun's National Theatre (Figure 8.2*f*). Lasdun's use of concrete surfaces and texture celebrates the sculptural possibilities of a material that in monolithic construction can perform many roles. The concrete profile echoes the tread-and-rise relationship while the stainless handrailing (bracketed off the solid balustrade) follows the awkward dictates of the by-laws without spoiling the overall form (as in Figure 8.2*d*).

Repetition in concrete stairs favours pre-casting the components. It is difficult to generalize but with high stair costs it is worth considering pre-cast manufacture that will simplify details into variants of Figures 8.2*b* and 8.2*c*.

Pre-cast stairs can be made in site factories (Figure 8.3*a*) and completed at this stage with a range of finishes (Figures 8.3*d–f*). Spine beam stairs are more

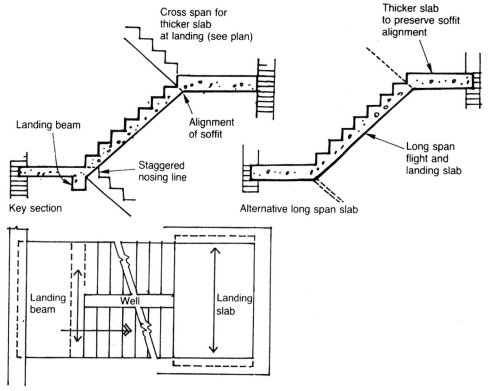

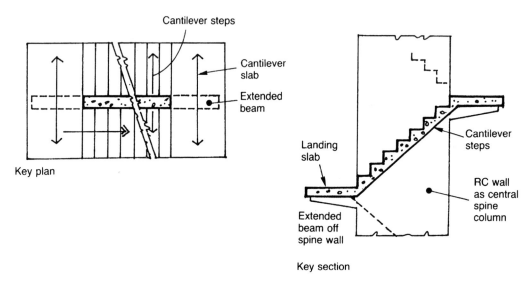

Figure 8.2a Developed forms of reinforced concrete stair: Simple RC slabs (with and without landing beams)

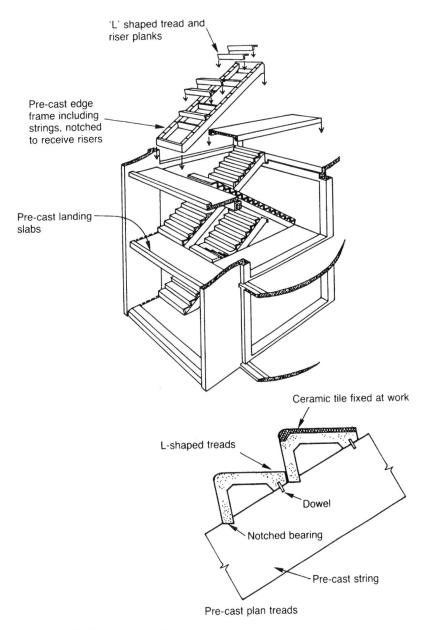

'L' shaped tread and riser planks

Pre-cast edge frame including strings, notched to receive risers

Pre-cast landing slabs

Ceramic tile fixed at work

L-shaped treads

Dowel

Notched bearing

Pre-cast string

Pre-cast plan treads

Figure 8.2b Pre-cast treads and beams

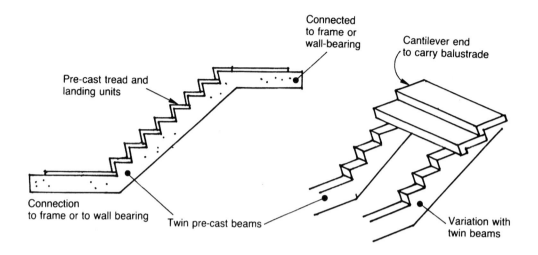

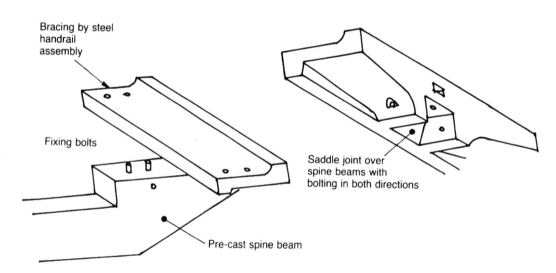

Figure 8.2c Spine beam support (with pre-cast treads)

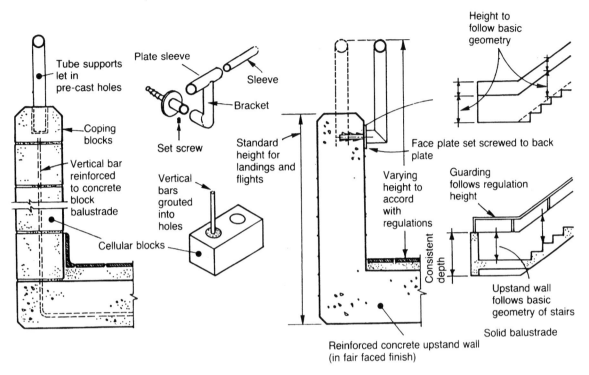

Figure 8.2d Balustrade upstand beams

efficient for long straight (Figures 8.3*b* and 8.3*c*) or curved flights due to the lower weight per span compared with solid slabs. Pre-cast assembly increasingly depends upon steel bolt and plate fastenings which demand the accuracy and connection methods associated with structural steelwork. Pre-cast reinforced treads are often cast with the finishes integral with the component; terrazzo can be used as a trowel coat within the mould and as a wearing coat to the tread, the final grinding and finishing following the curing stage. A spine wall can serve as a dog-leg column with cantilever action in the treads; by contrast the shaft walls can have cantilever steps leaving the well open for a metal balustrade.

The profile chosen by Ralph Erskine at Clare Hall, Cambridge, allows the carpet to be wrapped around the concrete treads, the rounded corners preventing wear and permitting the carpet to be turned from time to time. The reinforcing is tied into the backing wall which forms the shell-like enclosure (Figure 8.2*e*).

8.3 Pre-cast spiral stairs

The general arrangement of pre-cast spiral stairs is similar to steel spirals with tread units threaded over a central tubular column. The concrete profiles are more robust while finishes like terrazzo or tooled concrete (with stone aggregates or coloured cement) can produce surfaces as good as natural stonework. They look well externally (Figures 8.4*a–d*).

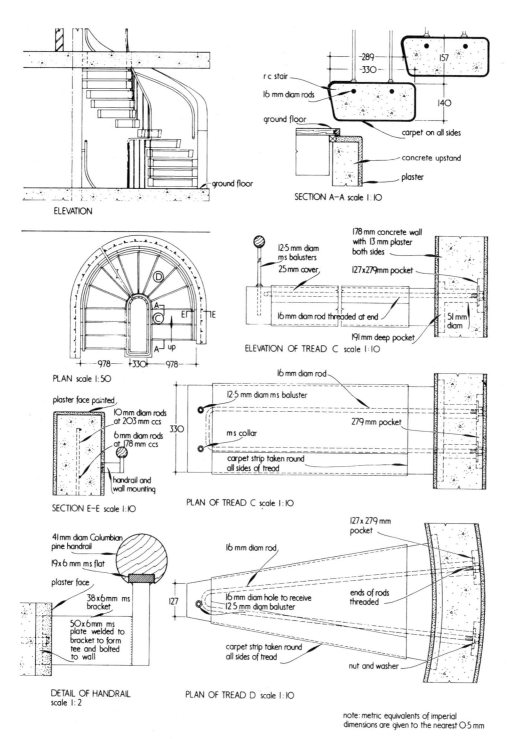

ELEVATION

SECTION A–A scale 1:10

- r c stair
- 16 mm diam rods
- ground floor
- carpet on all sides
- concrete upstand
- plaster

PLAN scale 1:50

ELEVATION OF TREAD C scale 1:10

- 12·5 mm diam ms balusters
- 25 mm cover
- 178 mm concrete wall with 13 mm plaster both sides
- 127 x 279 mm pocket
- 16 mm diam rod threaded at end
- 191 mm deep pocket
- 51 mm diam

SECTION E–E scale 1:10

- plaster face painted
- 10 mm diam rods at 203 mm ccs
- 6 mm diam rods at 178 mm ccs
- handrail and wall mounting

PLAN OF TREAD C scale 1:10

- 16 mm diam rod
- 12·5 mm diam ms baluster
- 279 mm pocket
- ms collar
- carpet strip taken round all sides of tread

DETAIL OF HANDRAIL scale 1:2

- 41 mm diam Columbian pine handrail
- 19 x 6 mm ms flat
- plaster face
- 38 x 6mm ms bracket
- 50 x 6mm ms plate welded to bracket to form tee and bolted to wall

PLAN OF TREAD D scale 1:10

- 127 x 279 mm pocket
- 16 mm diam rod
- 16 mm diam hole to receive 12·5 mm diam baluster
- ends of rods threaded
- carpet strip taken round all sides of tread
- nut and washer

note: metric equivalents of imperial dimensions are given to the nearest 0·5 mm

Figure 8.2e Cantilever concrete stairs, Clare Hall, Cambridge, 1969, Architect: Ralph Erskine (in association with Twist and Whitley)

Figure 8.2f Cast in-situ concrete work to stair shafts, Royal National Theatre, 1967–76, Architects: Denys Lasdun, Redhouse and Softley

Figure 8.3b Pre-cast beam stair prepared for tread fixing

Figure 8.3c Completed work with treads and balusters in place

Figure 8.3a Pre-cast stairs: Site factory at Wates Housing Development

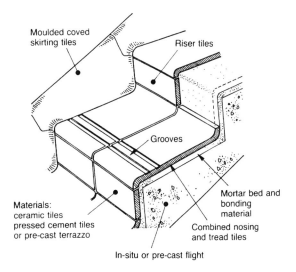

Moulded coved skirting tiles

Riser tiles

Grooves

Materials:
ceramic tiles
pressed cement tiles
or pre-cast terrazzo

Mortar bed and bonding material

Combined nosing and tread tiles

In-situ or pre-cast flight

Figure 8.3d Tile finished treads

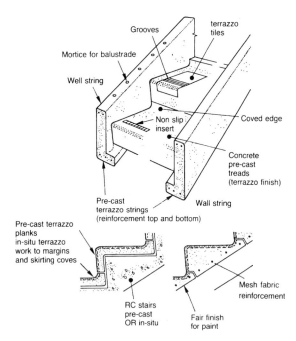

Figure 8.3e Terrazo finish

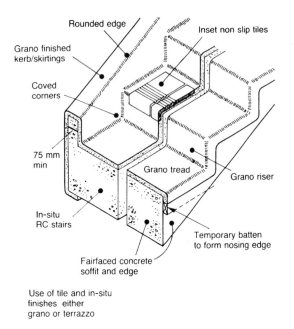

Figure 8.3f Combined finishes to treads

8.4 Detailing of well ends and balustrades

The solid profile of *in-situ* concrete stairs draws attention to the riser and well-end relationship. The appearance of sloping soffits and their bisection is of critical importance (Figures 8.5*a* and 8.5*b*) unless trimming beams or thicker slabs across the landing hide the junctions (Figure 8.5*c*). This may however appear clumsy. The alignments are compounded by the hand-rail-to-riser geometry, where 'slipping' the riser plane by one full step will improve matters (Figure 8.5*b*). It will be noted that the handrailing bisects in the same plane as the soffit and that no jump is incurred for the wreathing. In other words, the alignment gives 'slope to horizontal to slope' in the handrailing at well ends. By comparison, Figure 8.5*a* gives a vertical jump that is visually awkward.

Lengthening the well is another possibility with the use of a semicircle to set out handrail and well end. A well width equal to the tread will give a lift to the handrail in sympathy with the pitch to the flight (Figure 8.5*d*). A compromise which saves a few centimetres of space is the arrangement in Figure 8.5*e* where the riser plane is slipped by half a step. There are limitations, however, on aesthetic issues, particularly where a matching balustrade pattern is needed either side of the stairwell. In these circumstances non-conventional solutions such as solid fender walls or face-mounted railings will have to be explored (Figure 8.5*f*).

Generous layouts as in Figures 8.5*b* and 8.5*d* give better value in visual terms for both balustrade and well shape despite adding 250 mm (average tread) × stairhall width to the unlettable area of space.

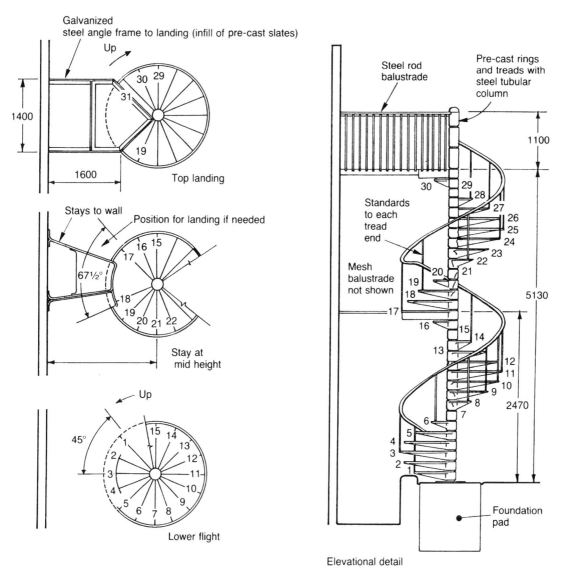

Figure 8.4a Pre-cast spiral stairs: Typical components using pre-cast treads and steel tubular column

Figure 8.4b Finished tread with terrazzo surface of different colours including non-slip insets

Figure 8.4d Context of artificial stone stairs set against stone work, Carcassone, 1870s

Figure 8.4c Artificial stone finish to spiral stair (courtesy of Cornish Spiral Stairs Ltd)

Metal balustrades to concrete stairs follow the principles laid down in Chapter 7, the differences arising if reinforced concrete fender spine walls are involved. The advantages of the latter rest with less metalwork to install and maintain. Figure 8.5g demonstrates Aalto's detailing at the Paimio Sanitorium as a superb example. The photograph was taken in 1968 when the original finishes were still intact. Another version of the concept could be made by using pre-cast terrazzo to the strings to receive the railings, with the flights also pre-cast with terrazzo tile finishes (Figure 8.5h).

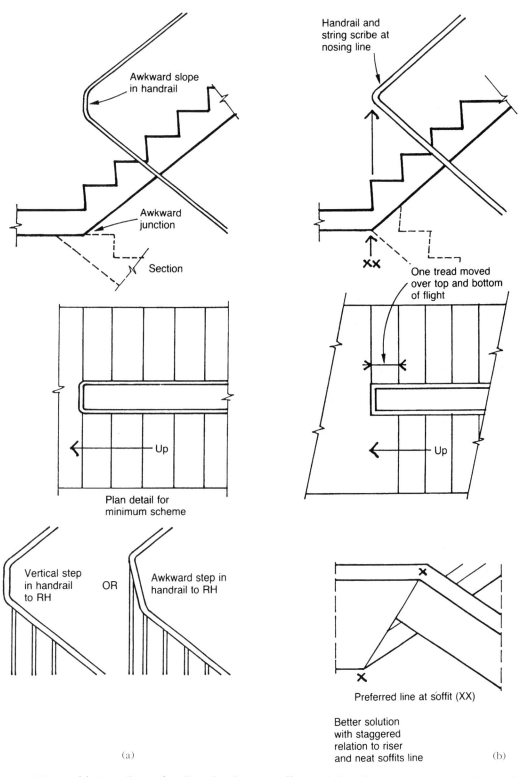

Figure 8.5a and b Detailing of well ends: Sloping soffits and their bisection, good and bad solutions

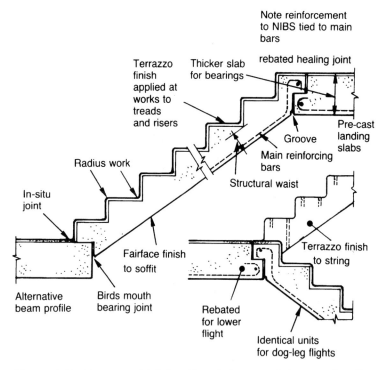

Note reinforcement to NIBS tied to main bars

Terrazzo finish applied at works to treads and risers

Thicker slab for bearings

rebated healing joint

Radius work

Groove

Pre-cast landing slabs

Main reinforcing bars

Structural waist

In-situ joint

Terrazzo finish to string

Fairface finish to soffit

Alternative beam profile

Birds mouth bearing joint

Rebated for lower flight

Identical units for dog-leg flights

Figure 8.5c Beam or thick landing slab to mask intersection lines

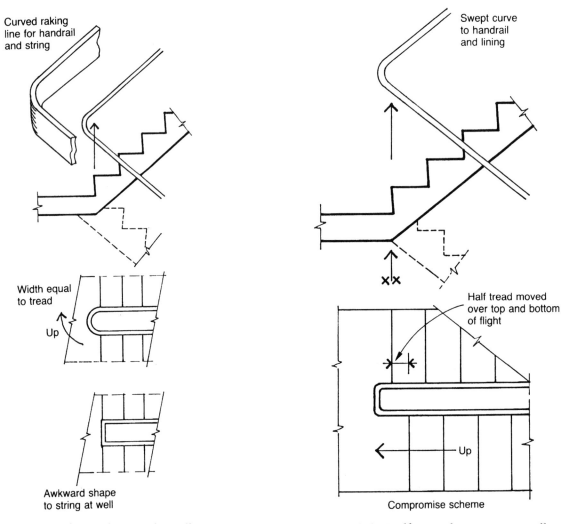

Curved raking line for handrail and string

Swept curve to handrail and lining

Width equal to tread

Up

x x

Half tread moved over top and bottom of flight

Up

Awkward shape to string at well

Compromise scheme

Figure 8.5d Lengthening the well

Figure 8.5e Half-step relation across well

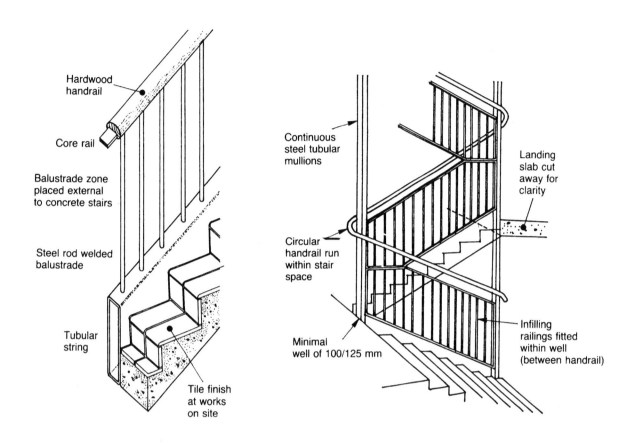

Hardwood handrail

Core rail

Balustrade zone placed external to concrete stairs

Steel rod welded balustrade

Tubular string

Tile finish at works on site

Continuous steel tubular mullions

Circular handrail run within stair space

Minimal well of 100/125 mm

Landing slab cut away for clarity

Infilling railings fitted within well (between handrail)

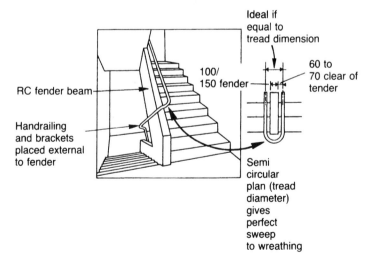

RC fender beam

Handrailing and brackets placed external to fender

100/ 150 fender

Ideal if equal to tread dimension

60 to 70 clear of tender

Semi circular plan (tread diameter) gives perfect sweep to wreathing

Figure 8.5f Face mounted railings

Figure 8.5g Fender walls with least balustrading, Paimio Sanitorium, Finland, 1933, Architect: Alvar Aalto

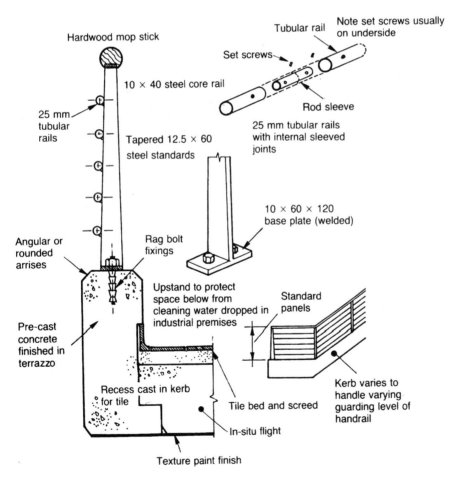

Figure 8.5h Fender in pre-cast terrazzo

9 Stonework and composite construction

Composite stair construction has already been mentioned with regard to steel and glass alongside steel and concrete, or steel working with timber. Traditional building methods relied on stonework slabs or vaulting or on stone cantilevers built in conjunction with iron balustrades.

9.1 Stonework in general terms

Chapter 2 touched upon stonework construction although it was primarily concerned with the systematic comparison of stairs. It is useful to list the types of construction and to cross reference these to the buildings illustrated in Chapter 2 alongside symbolic sketches in Figures 9.1*a–f* giving the principles involved.

- Stone slabs spanning enclosing walls.
- Stone blocks as a stylobate, namely stonework forming a stepped plinth, e.g. the steps to the Acropolis (Figure 9.1*b* and compare Figure 2.1*c*).

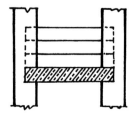

Figure 9.1a Principles for stonework stairs: Stone slabs spanning enclosing walls

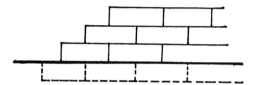

Figure 9.1b Principles for stonework stairs: Stone blocks as a stylobate

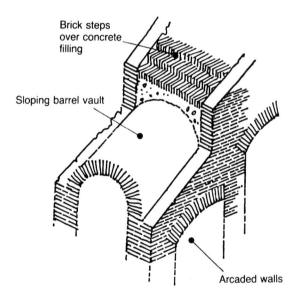

Figure 9.1c Principles for stonework stairs: Sloping barrel vault or sloping cross vault

- Stone vaults, either as a sloping barrel vault carried on walls or as cross vaults supported on columns, e.g. Palazzo Municipio, Genoa, or double circular stairs at Blois and Chambord (Figure 9.1*c* and compare Figures 2.11, 2.20 and 2.21).
- Turret stairs, with treads used as bonding stones between two independent towers (Figure 9.1*d*).

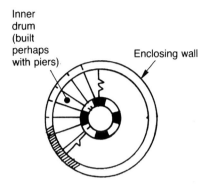

Figure 9.1d Principles for stonework stairs: Turret stairs with two independent towers

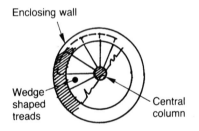

Figure 9.1e Principles for stonework stairs: Tapered threads with central column and enclosing wall

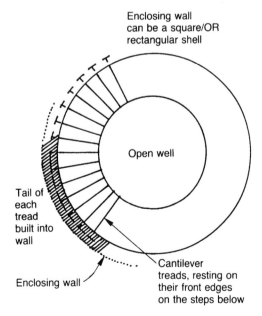

Figure 9.1f Principles for stonework stairs: Cantilevered stone stairs within a drum

● Turret stairs, with treads tapered and built up as a central newel or pier with tread ends built into the enclosing wall, for example, the stairs within corner piers at Chiswick House, London (refer back to Figure 2.18), or treads cantilevered out towards an open well (Figure 9.1*f*).

9.2 Turret and cantilevered stairs

One source for these dramatic structures of turret and cantilevered stairs is the influential writing of Andrea Palladio. The text from 1570 *I Quattro Libri del Architettura* (*The Four Books of Architecture*) devotes significant illustrations and text to the advantages of open well stairs constructed with stone cantilevers. The designs of Vignola's Palazzo Farnese, Caprarola, and Palladio's staircase in the Carita Monastery, Venice (Figures 9.2*a–c*), were both seen by Inigo Jones. In his sketchbooks, Jones records details of these stairs with notes as follows, 'They succeed very well that are void in the middle, because they can have light from above, and those that are at the top of stairs see all those that come up or begin to ascend, and are likewise seen by them'.

Inigo Jones certainly drew upon the inspiration of Andrea Palladio in the 'Tulip' staircase in the Queen's House, Greenwich (Figures 9.2*d* and 9.2*e*). A technical refinement occurred whereby the treads were rebated at the front bearing edge on the step below. The rebating prevented slipping in the building stage and improved the bearing from one tread to the next as compared with the

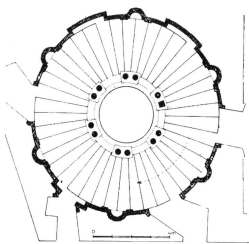

*Figure 9.2a Spiral stairs, Villa Farnese
(illustration and plan from Schuster, F.,* Treppen,
Homan Verlag, 1949)

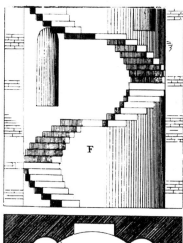

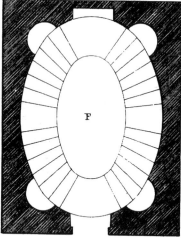

Figure 9.2c Detail of steps, Carita Monastery (from Ackerman, James S., Palladio, Penguin Books Ltd, 1979)

Figure 9.2b Turret and cantilever stairs: section plan of stairs at the Carita Monastery, Venice, 1560–61, Architect: Palladio

simple bed joint illustrated by Palladio (Figure 9.2c). Other notable English stairs built on the cantilever principle in the seventeenth or early eighteenth centuries are the open spirals at The Monument, City of London (Figure 9.2f), and the great stairs at Chatsworth (Figures 9.2g and 9.2h). Wren and Hooke deployed at The Monument a moulded riser, which features in full at the tapered end, while a blocked end to the nosing gives the necessary rebate at the tail of each tread. This detail is abandoned in the lower parts where a supporting wall exists towards the open well. A further development in

scale occurs with the geometrical stairs below the south-west tower stairs at St Paul's Cathedral, constructed by the master mason W. Kempster in 1706–8.

The most courageous cantilevers were made under Talman's direction at Chatsworth House, Derbyshire. The geometry follows a multiple-turn staircase within a square shaft. The cantilever dimension of 2 464 mm implies the cutting of vast blocks of sound local sandstone, the quarter landing slabs having sizes of around 2 600 mm². Each step weighed around 500 kg, the design above the first floor being reduced to more modest sizes of around 1 600 mm together with the introduction of carriage pieces. Talman was also involved with work at Hampton Court and it is thought likely that the modillion profile (Figure 9.2i) can be attributed to that source.

Figure 9.2d General view, Tulip staircase, Queen's House, Greenwich, 1629–35, Architect: Inigo Jones

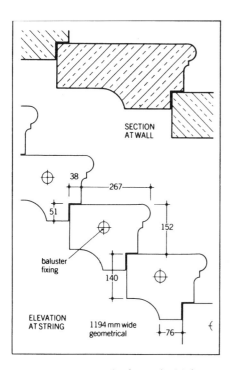

Figure 9.2e Detail of treads, Tulip staircase

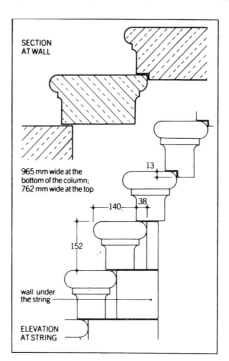

Figure 9.2f Details from cantilever steps, The Monument, City of London, circa 1671, Architects: Sir Christopher Wren and Robert Hooke

Figure 9.2g General view, The Great Stairs, Chatsworth House, Derbyshire, 1689–90, Architect: William Talman, balustrade by Tijou

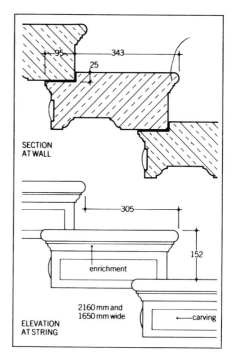

Figure 9.2h Detail of cantilever treads, The Great Stairs

The tailing-in of the tread ends is critical in terms of tightness of fit, the depth of bearing varying between 110 mm and 152 mm. The lesser dimension is common in nineteenth-century domestic work while Wren used 150 mm for the south-west tower stairs at St Paul's and 152 mm at Hampton Court. The crucial stabilizing role of the metal balustrade needs to be taken into account. Dismantling the balusters will often destabilize the treads. Such strengths may not be calculated but there is little doubt that stone cantilevers, and side-mounted balusters, act together once assembled with leaded joints from metal to stone (refer back to the Queen's House details, Figures 9.2d and 9.2e).

The moulding of the underside of the tread gives interest to the stair when viewed from below, as in the Da Costa House (Figure 9.2j). This is particularly important where both the up and down flights join a landing.

The beauty of the final example (Figure 9.3) is the sweeping soffit of the stair which gives a sculptural design to the entrance hall of this small house.

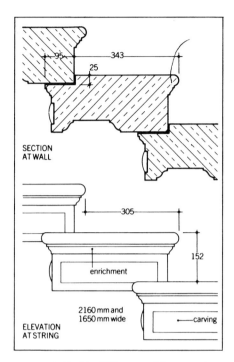

Figure 9.2i Modillion profile to stairs at Hampton Court, circa 1700

Figure 9.3 Stair showing sculptural form

Figure 9.2j General view, Da Costa House, Highgate, 1990, Architect: Russell Taylor, Engineer: Sam Price of Price and Myers

10 Design codes and procedures

The great problem in designing stairs is the strict rules laid down in the British Building Regulations, Approved Document K, 1998 edition, together with BS 5395. Although some reference to the Disabled Persons Act was included previously, it was only advisory. Since 1999, however, Approved Document M has made these provisions mandatory.

10.1 Key matters within the Building Regulations (including the 1997 and 1998 Amendments)

10.1.1 Application
The Regulations apply to stairs where the rise is greater than 600 mm. Outside stairs and ramps are not covered unless they form part of the building.

For access routes in assembly buildings, sports stadia etc. used for means of escape reference should be made to the following:

- BS 5588 Fire precautions in the design, construction and use of buildings, Part 6: 1991, Code of practice for places of assembly – for new assembly buildings.
- Guide to Fire Precautions in Existing Places of Entertainment and Like Premises, Home Office 1990 – for existing assembly buildings.
- Guide to Safety at Sports Grounds, The Stationery Office 1997 – for stands at sports grounds.

10.1.2 Intepretation
The Approved Document K represents an attempt to reorganize matters; these commence with standard definitions.

- *Containment* – a barrier to prevent people falling from a floor to the storey below.
- *Flight* – the section of a ramp or stair running between landings with a continuous slope or series of steps.
- *Ramp* – a slope which is steeper than 1 in 20 intended to enable pedestrians or wheelchair users to get from one floor level to another.
- *Stair* – steps and landings designed to enable pedestrians to get to different levels.
- *Private stairs* – stairs in or serving only one dwelling.
- *Institutional and assembly stairs* – stairs serving places where a substantial number of people gather.
- *Other stairs* – stairs serving all other buildings apart from those referred to above.
- *Going* – the distance measured in plan across the tread less any overlap with the next tread above (Figure 10.1*a*).
- *Rise* – the vertical distance between the top surfaces of two consecutive treads (Figure 10.1*a*).
- *Pitch line* – a notional line connecting the nosings of all treads in a flight. The line forms the greatest possible angle with the horizontal, subject to the special recommendations for tapered treads.

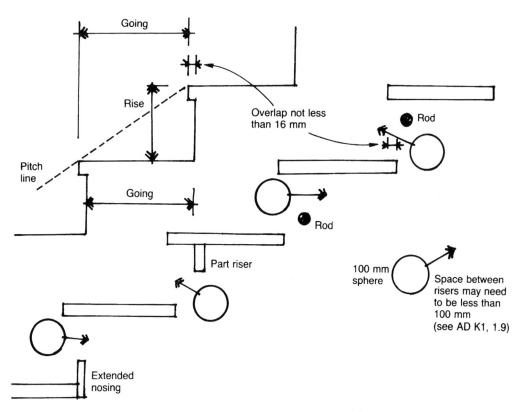

Figure 10.1a General requirements under Section K: Rise and going

- *Pitch* – the angle between the pitch line and horizontal (Figure 10.1*b*).
- *Alternative tread stairs* – stairs with paddle shaped treads where the wider portion alternates from one side to the other on each consecutive treads (Figure 10.1*d*).
- *Helical stairs* – stairs which form a helix round a central void.
- *Spiral stairs* – stairs which form a helix round a central column.
- *Ladder* – a series of rungs or narrow treads used as a means of access from one level to another which is normally used by a person facing the ladder.
- *Tapered tread* – a tread with a nosing which is not parallel to the nosing of the tread or landing above it.

10.1.3 General recommendations for stairways and ramps

- *Landings.* The going and width of the landing should not be less than the width of the flight or ramp. Landings should be level and free from permanent obstruction. A door is permitted to swing across a landing at the bottom of a flight if it leaves an area 400 mm wide across the width of stair or ramp.
- *Handrails.* Stairs and ramps should have a handrail on at least one side. Where the width is over 1 000 mm, then a handrail should be fixed on both sides.

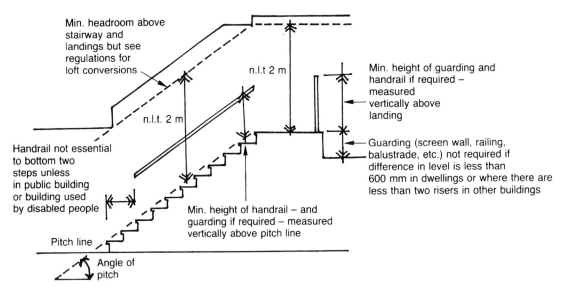

Figure 10.1b General requirements under Section K: section

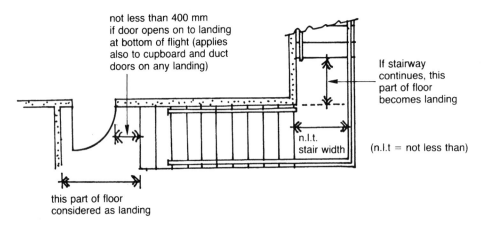

Figure 10.1c General requirements under Section K: plan

Handrails are not required:

- beside the bottom two steps in a stairway unless it is in a public building or intended for disabled people;
- where the rise of a ramp is 600 mm or less.
- Handrails to be between 900 mm and 1 000 mm.

Danger can occur by omitting the handrail for the last two steps – bad light or haste can precipitate a fall since the handhold and stair run are linked in the mind's eye. The Regulations recognize this danger for escape ramps and stairs and demand a handrail for the full length.

- *Headroom.* Clear headroom of 2 m should be provided over the whole width of any stairway, ramp or landing. Reduced headroom is allowed for loft conversions.

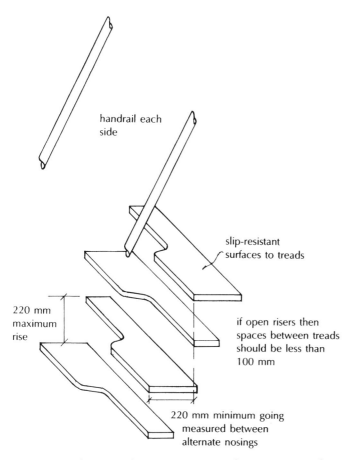

handrail each
side

slip-resistant
surfaces to treads

220 mm
maximum
rise

if open risers then
spaces between treads
should be less than
100 mm

220 mm minimum going
measured between
alternate nosings

Figure 10.1d General requirements under Section K: alternating tread stairs

Rise and going relationships have already been discussed in arriving at standard stairs for flats and commercial buildings in Chapter 3. The practical limits for the various building categories are given in Figures 10.1e–g. The pitch limitation should be noted (42° for private stairs, 35° for assembly and institutional buildings as well as common stairs).

10.1.4 Rules applying to all stairways

- In any stairway there should not be more than 36 rises in consecutive flights, unless there is a change in the direction of at least 30°.

- For any step the sum of twice its rise plus going $(2R + G)$ should not be more than 700 mm or less than 550 mm. This rule is subject to variation at tapered steps, for which there are special rules.

- The rise of any step should generally be constant throughout its length and all steps in a flight should have the same rise and going.

- Open risers are permitted in a stairway but for safety the treads should overlap each other by at least 16 mm and the space between be not more than 100 mm.

- Each tread in a stairway should be level.

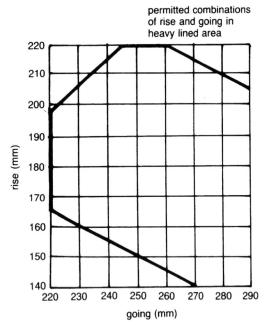

Figure 10.1e General requirements under Section K: Practical limits (rise and going) – private stairways

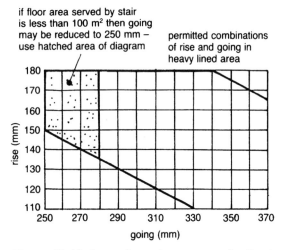

Figure 10.1f General requirements under Section K: Practical limits (rise and going) – institutional and assembly buildings

10.1.5 Tapered treads should comply with the following rules

(Figure 10.1*h*)

- The minimum going at any part of a tread within the width of a stairway should not be less than 50 mm.

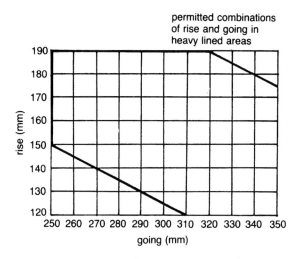

Figure 10.1g General requirements under Section K: Practical limits (rise and going) – other buildings

- The going should be measured:
  (i) if the stairway is less than 1 m wide, at the centre point of the length or deemed length of a tread, and
  (ii) if a stairway is 1 m or more wide, at points 270 mm from each end of the length or deemed length of a tread. (When referring to a set of consecutive tapered treads of different lengths, the term 'deemed length' means the length of the shortest tread.)
- All consecutive tapered treads in a flight should have the same taper.
- Where stairs contain straight and tapered treads the goings of the tapered treads should not be less than those of the straight flight.

10.1.6 Rules applying to private stairways

- The height of any rise should not be more than 220 mm.
- The going of any step should not be less than 220 mm (excluding tapered treads).
- The pitch should not be more than 42°.

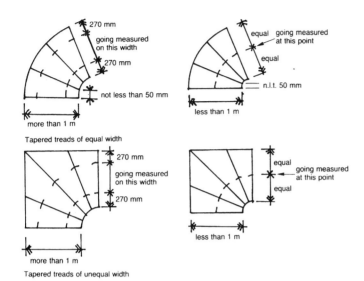

Tapered treads of equal width

Tapered treads of unequal width

Figure 10.1b General requirements under Section K: Tapered treads

10.1.7 Rules applying to institutional and assembly stairs

Often used by children, the elderly or disabled, these stairs need to have a lower pitch.

- Rise 180 mm maximum and going 280 mm minimum (excluding tapered treads) but can be reduced to 250 mm if the floor area is less than 100 m².

- In order to maintain sight lines for spectators in assembly buildings gangways can be pitched at 35°.

10.1.8 Widths of stairs

The Regulations in Section K no longer have specific rules on the widths of stairs, but Section B for fire safety and Section M for access and facilities for the disabled specify some minimum widths. The practical problems of handling furniture need to be considered, tight turns can restrict the movement. Access to bathrooms and WCs can be reduced to 600 mm.

Section B, Fire Regulations and Section M, Disabled Facilities have restrictions.

The key dimensions for stair widths are given as follows.

- The narrowest permitted escape stair is 800 mm.
- Common stairs in flats have to be 1 000 mm but 1 100 mm if they are fire fighting stairs.
- A stair serving an assembly building has to be 1 000 mm unless the area served is less than 100 m².
- Stairs that are wider than 1 800 mm in assembly buildings have to be divided by guard rails.
- Stair widths are measured at 1 500 mm height.
- The widths depend upon the number of persons in the building (Figure 10.1*i*).
- The Regulations assume that in buildings with two escape routes one will be disabled by fire. The widths for each stair have to conform with the tables (Figures 10.1*i* and 10.1*j*) since either may have to take the full traffic load in an emergency.

Maximum number of persons	Minimum width (mm)
50	800[3]
110	900
220	1100
more than 220	5 per person

Figure 10.1i Widths of escape routes and exit

Maximum number of people in any storey	Stair width[1] (mm)
100	1000
120	1100
130	1200
140	1300
150	1400
160	1500
170	1600
180	1700
190	1800

Notes:
1. Stairs with a rise of more than 30 m should not be wider than 1400 mm unless provided with a central handrail (see para 4.6 [p.7.55]).
2. As an alternative to using this table, provided that the minimum width of a stair is at least 1000 mm, the width may be calculated from: (P×10) – 100] mm where P = the number of people on the most heavily occupied storey.

Figure 10.1j General requirements under Section K: Minimum aggregate width of stairs designed for phased evacuation

- Long flights over 30 m in descent to be 1 400 mm maximum width, which implies a total traffic limit of 700 persons per stair.
- Stairs over 1 400 mm wide may have to jump to 1 800 mm wide to comply with the central guard-rail rule.
- Phased evacuation permits narrower stairs since safe collection points have to be provided at various floor locations in the height of the building (Figure 10.1j). In buildings planned for phased evacuation each floor must be a compartment floor, stairs must relate to a protected lobby or passage approach, a fire warning system and intercom is needed between fire wardens (floor by floor) and a control point. Sprinklers are required

throughout buildings which exceed 30 m in height.

- Stairs used for means of escape in case of fire must exit direct to the open air.
- The Regulations permit strings and handrails to project into the stair width (Figure 10.1k).

The Regulations are very specific about forms of lifts and stairs that are not acceptable as means of escape in case of fire.

- Lifts unless evacuation lifts.
- Portable or throwaway ladders.
- Fold-down ladders.
- Escalators (though travelators are accepted if switched off in case of fire).
- Accommodation stairs (except for small shops with a total area of all floors less than 90 m^2 and limited to basement, ground and first floor level).

10.1.9 Stairs to loft conversions

Headroom. Where there is insufficient height to achieve the recommended 2 m over a stairway, 1.9 m at the centre of the stair is acceptable reducing to 1.8 m at the side.

10.1.10 Ladders

Fixed ladders may be installed for access in a loft conversion where there is insufficient room to install a conventional stair without alteration to the existing space, if they conform to the following:

- There should be fixed handrails on both sides.
- The ladder should only serve one habitable room.

Retractable ladders are not acceptable for means of escape in case of fire.

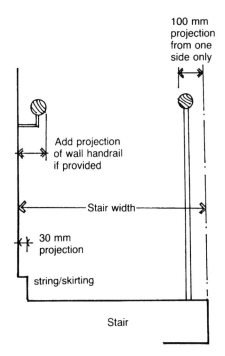

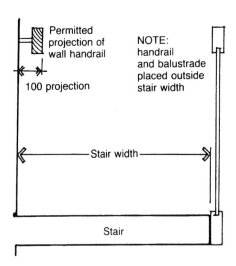

Figure 10.1k General requirements under Section K: Handrail projection into stair widths

10.1.11 Spiral and helical stairs

Must conform with BS 5395 Stairs, ladders and walkways, Part 2: 1984, Code of practice for the design of helical and spiral stairs.

10.1.12 Alternating tread stairs
(Figure 10.1*d*)

Now allowed providing they conform to the following:

- are in one or more straight flights;
- provide access to only one habitable room plus bathroom or WC provided it is not the only WC in the dwelling;
- are fitted with handrails on both sides;
- contain treads with slip-resistant surfaces;
- have uniform steps with parallel nosings;
- have a minimum going of 220 mm and a maximum rise of 220 mm when measured over the wider part of the tread;
- conform to the recommendations regarding maximum gap for open rise treads, 100 mm.

10.2 Ramps and guarding of stairs etc.

The categories for the use of ramps are similar to those set down for stairways, the width not being less than that required for the same category of stair.

- The slope of any ramp should not be more than 1 in 12.
- There should be no permanent obstructions placed across any ramp.

Vehicle ramps or areas of buildings accessible by vehicles are required to have barriers in order to protect people.[1] Document K2/3 in the Regulations provides guidance on barriers and is shown in Figure 10.2.

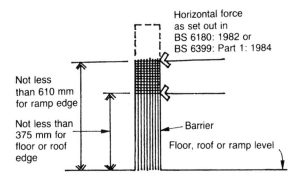

Figure 10.2 Vehicle barriers (ramps, etc.)

10.3 Means of escape in case of fire (general matters under Building Regulations)

The National Building Regulations make general provisions on access and exit matters and these can be enumerated as follows:

- *1984 Act, Section 24: Access and Exit.* This section governs access and exit in public buildings and places of public assembly as well as those licensed for entertainment, music and dance. The fire authority has to agree the details: disputes can be determined by the Magistrates' Court.
- *1984 Act, Sections 6 and 7: Deposit of Plans.* Sections 6 and 7 require deposit of plans that show the intended arrangement and stipulate that plans shall be updated to show what has been finally built and agreed.
- *Local legislation.* Many local authorities have created special powers relevant to building control and these should be checked. Under these local provisions there often exist extra safety requirements for basement garages, e.g. the lobby approach to stairs. Another com-

mon requirement is that buildings in excess of 18.3 m height have fire alarm systems and that adequate access exists for the fire brigade to reach lifts and stairs.
- *1984 Act: Means of Escape above 6 or 4.5 metres.* This provision covers escape stairs where there is a storey over 6 or 4.5 m above ground in specific buildings, namely hotels, boarding houses and hospitals.

10.4 Buildings of excess height and excess cubical content

Such buildings are still governed within inner London by Section 20 of the London Building (Amendment) Act 1939. The provisos affect buildings higher than 30 m, or 25 m if the area of the building exceeds 930 m^2, or for large trade buildings over 7 100 m^3. The means of escape in case of fire under Section 20 are still controlled by Sections 33 and 34 of the 1939 Act. The requirements are more stringent than those in Code of Practice 3 clause IV or in BS 5588.[2]

10.5 Mandatory rules for means of escape in case of fire

The mandatory rules are prescribed in Part B of Schedule 1 to the Building Regulations (1991), known as Approved Document B1. These relate to fire compartments, sprinklers, etc. and should be checked carefully.[3] As they do not apply to the actual design of stairs they have been omitted in this edition.

Indication of these rules in practice are given in Chapter 3 (Figures 3.4*a* and 3.4*b*). The numbers refer to clauses in Approved Document B1. Full information can be obtained from the latest edition of *The Easiregs* prepared by Henry Haverstock for Building Design.[4]

10.6 Escape from flats

Ground and first floor flats are treated as houses, assuming occupants can jump from first floor windows. Flats above second floor are subject to mandatory rules as summarized in Figures 10.3*a* and 10.3*b*. Protected hallways within flats are limited to 9 m in length. Flats planned more spaciously will need alternative means of escape to balconies and secondary stairs, which can be external but are limited to 6 m unless protected from snow and ice. Internal escapes should terminate at ground level.

10.7 Escape from offices (BS 5588: Part 3, Codes of Practice for Office Buildings)

The horizontal escape is limited by travel distances (Figures 10.4*a–c*) which refer to all levels (ground and upwards). The number of exits is calculated by occupancy, see Figure 10.4*d*.

Escape stairs have to be duplicated in the following circumstances.

- Buildings of three or less storeys.

- For building heights not greater than 11 m (measured from top floor to the lowest ground level adjacent to the building).

A typical vertical core is shown in Figure 10.4*e*. Lobbies cannot be used as through routes to other stairs unless subdivided by fire doors.

10.8 New technology

Today's technology for fire protection includes smoke detectors, linked to automatic door release and which overcomes the annoyance of the lobby approach to stairs in high-risk locations. Today the stair enclosure doors will operate on a self-closing device whilst the second set of doors will be released by electromagnets. A further change is the acceptance of positive air pressure within the escape routes and stairhalls to expel smoke that may enter from adjacent accommodation. The Loss Prevention Council is a useful authority on up-to-date procedures.[5] They publish a number of guides and advise on fire-fighting facilities.

10.9 Access and facilities for disabled people

Although recommendations for disabled people were included in the previous Regulations, they were not obligatory, but under the 1998 revision to Approved Document M new regulations came into force on 25 October 1999. When dealing with access requirements for disabled people reference should also be made to the Disability Discrimination Act 1995.

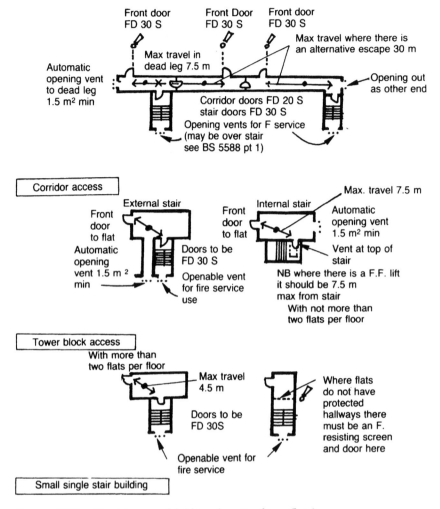

Figure 10.3a Corridors and lobbies (escape from flats)

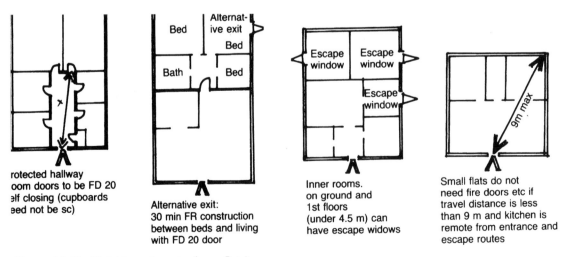

Figure 10.3b Flat plans (escape from flats)

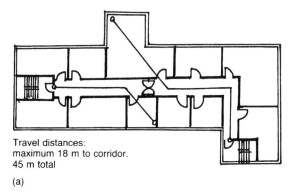

Travel distances:
maximum 18 m to corridor.
45 m total

(a)

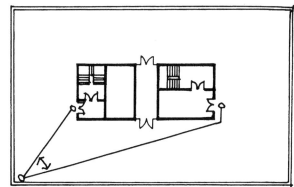

Direct distances – central core
maximum 12 m if angle is less than 45°

(b)

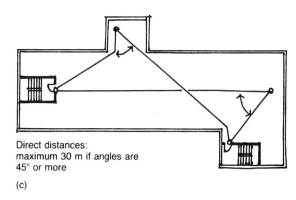

Direct distances:
maximum 30 m if angles are
45° or more

(c)

Maximum number of persons	Minimum number of escape routes/exits
500	2
1000	3
2000	4
4000	5
7000	6
11000	7
16000	8
more than 16000	8

(d) Table for number of escape routes

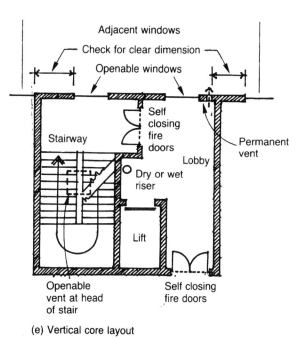

(e) Vertical core layout

Figure 10.4 Escape from offices

From the viewpoint of construction work, after 2004 service providers will have to ensure that there are no physical features which make it unreasonably difficult for disabled people to use their services. For example, this may involve installing accessible entrances, lifts, etc., in existing buildings. The Regulations apply to:

- New buildings.
- Extensions to existing buildings (but not to dwellings, which are excluded from Approved Document M) if the extension has a ground storey. The extension must comply with the requirements of Approved Document M but there is no obligation to bring the existing building up to standard. If the extension is capable of being independently approached and entered from the boundary of the site, then it should be treated as if it were a new building.

10.9.1 The main provisions for buildings other than dwellings

- Provision for the disabled to enter and use their facilities, and sanitary accommodation.
- A reasonable number of wheelchair spaces, where the building contains audience or spectator seating.

10.9.2 Means of access, approach to the building

- Access should be provided to the entrance and from the car park on the level or by a ramp no steeper than 1 in 20.
- The width of entrance to be 1 200 mm.
- Tactile pavings to be provided for people with impaired vision where the route crosses vehicle access.

10.9.3 Ramped access

- Should have a non-slip surface.
- Ideally, should not be steeper than 1 in 20. However, a 1 in 15 ramp is permitted if the individual flight is no longer than 10 m. Similarly a 1 in 12 ramp is allowed where the flight does not exceed 5 m in length.
- Should have a landing top and bottom at least 1 200 mm long, clear of any door swing.
- Should have intermediate landings at least 1 500 mm long, clear of any door swing.
- Should have on any open side of a flight or landing a raised kerb at least 100 mm high. This helps to avoid the risk to wheelchair users of their feet catching under or in an open balustrade.
- Should have a width of at least 1 200 mm.
- Should have handrails on both sides if the ramp is over 2 m long.

10.9.4 Lifts

Lifts should be provided to serve any floor above or below the principal entrance storey where the following nett floor areas are exceeded:

- Two-storey buildings – 280 m^2 of nett floor area.
- Buildings exceeding two storeys – 200 m^2 of nett floor area.

Where passenger lifts are not provided a stair suitable for ambulant disabled people should be provided.

A suitable lift design is shown in Figure 10.5. Its main features are:

- An unobstructed, accessible landing space at least 1 500 m^2 in front of the lift.

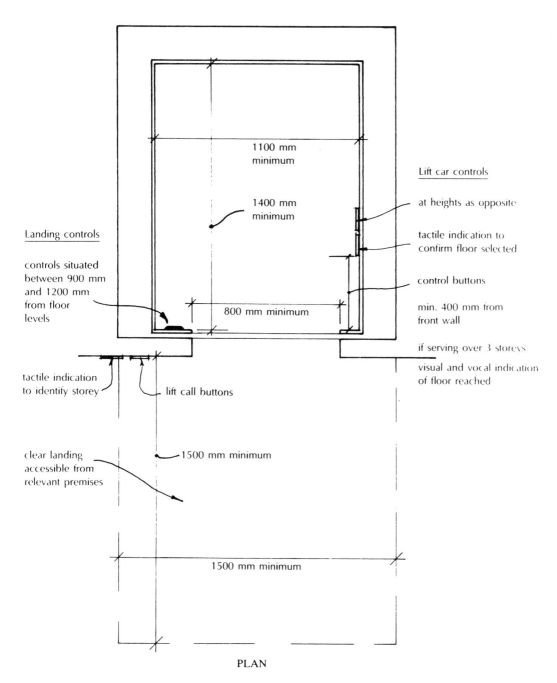

Lift car controls

at heights as opposite

tactile indication to
confirm floor selected

control buttons

min. 400 mm from
front wall

if serving over 3 storeys:

visual and vocal indication
of floor reached

1100 mm
minimum

1400 mm
minimum

Landing controls

controls situated
between 900 mm
and 1200 mm
from floor
levels

800 mm minimum

tactile indication
to identify storey

lift call buttons

clear landing
accessible from
relevant premises

1500 mm minimum

1500 mm minimum

PLAN

Figure 10.5 Lift (suitable for disabled people)

- A door or doors with a clear opening width of 800 mm.
- A car with minimum dimensions of 1 100 mm wide by 1 400 mm deep.
- Landing and car controls between 900 mm and 1 400 mm from landing or car floor levels and at least 400 mm from front wall.
- Tactile floor level indication where the lift serves more than three floors, on or adjacent to the lift buttons in the lift car to confirm the floor selected.
- Visual and vocal floor indication where the lift serves more than three floors.
- A signalling system which gives a five-second warning that the lift is about to stop at a floor and, once stopped, a minimum of five seconds before the doors begin to close after being fully open.

10.9.5 Stairlifts and platform lifts

Stairlifts and platform lifts described in Chapter 11 can be used but must conform to BS 5776: 1996 Specification for powered stairlifts, and BS 6440: 1983 Code of practice for powered lifting platforms for use by disabled people.

10.9.6 Internal stairways

Where a lift is not provided in a building then a stairway suitable for ambulent disabled people or those with impaired sight should be provided. The principal variations permitted are:

- Uniform risers should not exceed 170 mm in height
- Uniform goings should not be less than 250 mm in length (measured 270 mm in from the narrow edge of the flight for tapered steps).

- Stair nosings should be distinguished for the benefit of people with impaired sight.
- The maximum rise of a flight between landings should not exceed 1 800 mm.

10.10 American codes

The final part of this chapter (paragraphs 10.10.1 to 10.10.6) has been prepared by Ian Smith ARIBA AIA, a British architect who has been working in New York for more than 30 years. He reviews two codes that apply in the eastern and western parts of the USA and which have the advantage of brevity.

10.10.1 A review of code requirements governing stairs and ramps in the USA

The United States of America has a population of over 250 million, has a land mass twice the size of Europe and is divided into 50 separate states, each of which jealously guards its right to establish its own laws. It can therefore be hardly surprising that, throughout the country, a great number of different building codes are in force.

The larger cities all impose their own codes which, being written by lawyers, are provided with enough built-in contradictions to keep their framers in business. The New York City code, for example, is so opaque and so resistant to rational interpretation that a new type of professional has been created to deal with it; part architect, part engineer, part lawyer known as an 'expediter'. For a hefty fee the expediter shepherds the architect's drawings through the arcane workings of the borough building departments, surfacing from time to time with necessary pieces of documentation; emerging finally with the certificate of occupancy in hand.

Most smaller towns and cities, however, have found it expedient to adopt one of the two National Codes that have now been widely used for many years, both of which provide a consulting and inspection service. These codes are:

- *The Uniform Building Codes.*
  First enacted by the International Conference of Building Officials in Phoenix, Arizona in 1927. Their present headquarters are in Whittier, California.
- *The BOCA National Building Code.*
  Published by the Building Officials and Code Administrators International, Inc. (BOCA), first enacted in 1950. Their present headquarters are in Chicago, Illinois, with regional offices in Columbus, Ohio, Tulsa, Oklahoma and Trevose, Pennsylvania.

In very broad terms it can be said that the Uniform Building Code is favoured west of the Mississippi River, the BOCA National Building Code to its east.

For the purpose of this review the BOCA code will be discussed, with comments on the UBC in those areas where there is a significant divergence from BOCA. The summaries are based largely upon stair requirements for commercial buildings.

10.10.2 Planning principles governing the number and location of exit stairways

The following review is restricted to 'required' stairs: that is to say, stairs used exclusively for the evacuation of a floor to the open air at ground level, contained within a fire-rated enclosure.

The location and number of legally required exit stairs from any floor is determined by the total occupancy of the floor, the distance of travel from any point on the floor to the nearest stair, and the basic principle that stairs should be remote one from another.

The occupancy of the floor is calculated by referring to a table that sets out the maximum floor area allowance per occupant for a wide range of uses. The allowance for a usage not specifically included in the table may be determined by negotiation with the building official.

Once the occupancy has been determined the minimum of stairways is calculated as in Figure 10.6.

The second factor determining the number of stairs required is the limitation of the distance of travel (measured as an exact path of travel) from any point on the floor nearest a stair or fire-rated corridor leading to a stair. This distance varies in accordance with usage and whether or not the space is served by sprinklers. For example, in such general usages as assembly, business, mercantile or educational, the maximum path of travel distance is 250 ft (76 m) if the space has sprinklers and 200 ft (61 m) if it has not. Hospitals are more restricted; warehouses less. The final planning

Occupancy load	Minimum number of stairs
500 or less	2
501–1000	3
Over 1000	4

Figure 10.6 Calculation of minimum number of stairways

restraint is the doctrine of 'remoteness' which governs the location of stairs in relation to one another. The rule states that where only two stairs are required they should be no closer (when measured in a straight line) than half of a straight line connecting the two most remote corners of the space. The distance of separation may be halved if the space is sprinklered; a concession, it should be noted, that is not allowed in the Uniform Building Code.

In large floors where more than two stairs are required the rule governing path of travel ensures that stairs are well separated, but in any case the code inspector will insist on a reasonable distribution of stairs.

Width of stairs

Having calculated the number of stairs it is now necessary to calculate the total stair width. This is, of course, directly related to the occupancy of the floor. The method of calculation, however, varies radically between BOCA and UBC and I will therefore review both.

Stair width calculation, BOCA Code

The total stair width is calculated by using a *unit width* multiplied by the number of occupants. The unit width varies from use to use and is significantly less when the space is sprinklered. For example:

a   For general use such as assembly, business, educational, mercantile, residential, storage or manufacture the unit width is 0.2 in (5 mm) if the space is sprinklered, and 0.3 in (7.5 mm) if not.

b   In hospitals the unit width is 0.3 in (7.5 mm) if sprinklered and 1 in (25 mm) if not.

Exit stair width is calculated for the *occupancy of the floor only*, that is to say, the stair 'load' *is not cumulative.*

Stair width calculations using UBC

Total stair width is calculated by dividing the total occupancy by 50, expressing the result in feet. No distinction is made between use groups and no concessions are granted for sprinklered floors.

The major difference between BOCA and UBC however is that UBC calculates the stair loading in a multi-storey building on a *cumulative basis*. The rule is that the stair must accommodate 50 per cent of the load of the floor immediately above plus 25 per cent of load of the floor above that.

It is therefore immediately clear that in a building of more than two floors UBC is a much stricter code than BOCA. As a practical matter, however, the different ways of calculating stair width do not become a design issue until the floor occupancy reaches a little over 200; as for example, in a multi-storey office building with a uniform single floor area of 20 000 ft^2 (1 860 m^2). In a floor of this size BOCA requires a total stair width of 60 in (1 524 mm) while UBC (bearing in mind that the load is cumulative) requires a width of 84 in (2 134 mm). Both are therefore still below the mandated minimum requirement of two stairs of 44 in width each, i.e. 88 in (2 235 mm).

The UBC requirements do become onerous, however, in buildings such as department stores where an upper floor occupancy is often as high as 1 500 persons.

10.10.3 Detailed design of stairways

a *Width*

No stair may be less than 44 in (1 118 mm) wide. All stairs from a floor should be approximately the same width to achieve an even distribution of exiting load.

b *Landings*

The landings must be the same width as the stairs, except that landings connecting flights in a straight run need not be more than 48 in (1 219 mm).

c *Headroom*

Clear headroom measured vertically from the nosing of a stair or floor landing must not be less than 6 ft 8 in (2 032 mm).

d *Vertical rise*

Maximum vertical rise between landings or intermediate platforms: 12 ft (3 658 mm).

e *Treads and risers*

There are no regulations regarding pitch.

Maximum riser: 7 in (178 mm)

Minimum riser: 4 in (102 mm)

Minimum going: 11 in (279 mm)

No winders allowed.

f *Handrails*

Handrails should present a continuous gripping surface without obstructions such as newels. There must be a clear $1\frac{1}{2}$ in (38 mm) from rail to wall and the rail may project into the stair a maximum of $3\frac{1}{2}$ in (88 mm). The rail must be no more than 38 in (965 mm) above the stair nosing or landing floor and no less than 34 in (864 mm).

Handrail ends must continue horizontally at least 12 in (305 mm) beyond the top nosing of a flight. At the bottom of a flight the handrail must continue at the same slope for the equivalent of one tread beyond the bottom nosing and then continue horizontally for a minimum of 12 in (305 mm).

Intermediate handrails are required so that no part of a stair is more than 30 in (762 mm) from a handrail.

g *Guardrails*

In educational buildings the guard rails at stairs and landings should not be less than 42 in (1 067 mm). In all other use groups, minimum height: 34 in (864 mm). Open guards (i.e. open balustrades) should have balusters or other construction that will not pass a 4 in (102 mm) sphere.

10.10.4 General notes

The foregoing review has covered the rules governing the location, size and detail of the stairs themselves. Very specific rules also govern the sizes of the corridors or aisles leading to the stairs, the doors that open into the stairways and the doors that exit from them.

Aisles and corridors

An aisle (as in a department store for example) or corridor leading to any stair must be at least wide enough to match the capacity of the stair it serves.

Doors

Stair access doors must open in the direction of travel, i.e. into the stair enclosure. When doors are fully open they may intrude into the landing space no more than 7 in (178 mm).

Doors must be self-closing, be unlocked but equipped with a latch that will open automatically under pressure, and have a fire rating matching that of the enclosure. Doors exiting from stairs must be equipped with panic hardware. All doors, in or out, must be a minimum width of 32 in (813 mm) and match the capacity of the stair.

Stair enclosures

All stairs required as a legal means of egress must be constructed of non-combustible materials and must be within a fire-rated enclosure. For buildings of more than four floors the rating is generally 2 hours; 1 hour if less. A 2-hour fire rating can be achieved with an assembly comprising 6 in (152 mm) galvanized metal studs with two layers of 5/8 in (16 mm) 'fire code' gypsum board (equal to Fireline board) on each side.

Lighting

All stairs must be equipped with an emergency lighting system. In smaller buildings the system may be energized by battery packs; in large buildings, such as hospitals and department stores, a generator set that kicks in immediately upon the failure of electrical service, is required.

10.10.5 Domestic stairs

Stairs inside houses or apartments are, of course, much less restricted than legally required exit stairs. They need not be enclosed, risers may be a maximum of $8\frac{1}{4}$ in (210 mm) and the 'going' a minimum of 9 in (229 mm). Spiral stairs and winders are also permitted with some dimensional restrictions.

10.10.6 Ramps

The Americans With Disabilities Act of 1990 became effective on 26 January 1992. Its provisions, in the form of guidelines for the design of new buildings and for retro-fitting old ones, are not yet part of any building code. However, non-compliance with the Act's provision leaves the building owner open to suit on the grounds of discrimination on the basis of disability. The owner of an existing building is obliged to do everything possible to comply with ADA but it is recognized that some of the Act's requirements are not achievable. In new construction, however, no such excuse is possible and non-compliance opens up the very real possibilities of a suit being brought against all those associated with a project: owner, architect and contractors.

ADA is a Federal Act and is applicable in every state. In dealing with this section therefore, UBC and BOCA have been put aside for a review of ADA rules and regulations.

a   *Slope and rise*
    Maximum slope shall be: 1 in 12
    Maximum rise between landings shall be: 30 in (760 mm)
b   *Clear width*
    Minimum clear width shall be: 36 in (915 mm)
c   *Landings*
    Level landings shall be provided at the top and bottom of each ramp run.
    Landings shall have a length of 60 in (1 525 mm) clear, and if the ramp changes direction at the landing the minimum size shall be 60 in × 60 in (1 525 mm × 1 525 mm).
    Doorways at landings shall have a flat

area in front of the door (in its closed position) of 60 in (1 525 mm).

d *Handrails*

If the rise of the ramp is over 6 in handrails must be provided on both sides. If handrails are not continuous they shall extend 12 in horizontally beyond the end of the ramp. Handrails shall be 34–38 in (865–965 mm) above the ramp landing.

e *Edge protection*

Ramps and landings with drop-offs shall have a minimum 2 in (50 mm) curb below in addition to standards supporting the handrails to prevent wheelchairs from sliding off the ramp.

References

1 For greater detail on vehicle barriers refer to BS 6189 (1982) Code of Practice for protective barriers in and about buildings. These cover circumstances where vehicles weigh more than 2.5 tonnes or are moving at greater speeds than 16 km/hour.

2 BS 5588 Fire precautions in the design, construction and use of buildings:

Part 1: Residential buildings
Part 2: Shops
Part 3: Office buildings
Part 4: Smoke control
Part 5: Fire fighting stairways and lifts
Part 6: Assembly buildings
Part 7: Atrium buildings
Part 9: Ventilation and air conditioning ductwork
Part 10: Enclosed shopping complexes

3 Home Office and other ministerial publications:
  • *Home Office guide to fire precautions in existing places of entertainment*, Home Office, 1990.
  • *DHSS Firecode*, Health and Social Security, HMSO, 1987.
  • *DES Building Bulletin 7*, Fire and design of educational buildings, HMSO, 1988.
  • *Home Office guide to safety at sports grounds*, Home Office/Scottish Office, HMSO, 1990.

4 *Easiregs* – the latest collection of this valuable guidance is titled *Easibrief* and was published for Building Design by Morgan-Grampion (Construction Press) Ltd, 1993. Many of the figures in this chapter have been redrawn from this source, courtesy of Henry Haverstock.

5 The Loss Prevention Council, 140 Aldersgate Street, London EC1A 4HY.

11 Elevators and mechanical circulation

11.1 Introduction

The topic of machines for moving people is a manual in itself. The mechanical means, whether elevator (lift, escalator), moving stairs or travelator have revolutionized the planning of buildings, and have in many ways eclipsed the role of staircases. Without lifts the development of the skyscraper would not have been possible. This chapter reviews the historical development in the mechanics of shifting people up and down or through a building. The material presented owes a great deal to the help given by Kevan Goetch and Barry Wheeler from Otis Elevator plc.

Readers wanting precise information on the sizing of elevators, together with lift rooms etc. and escalators, need to turn to the industry itself, which operates a design service that covers traffic calculation, number and size of equipment as well as advice on motive power.

11.2 Historical review

A fascinating book published by the Otis Elevator Company, *Going Up*, in 1983 traces the history in detail with wonderful drawings of early hoists and lifts.[1] That history is described with illustrations in *Stairs, Steps and Ramps*. Sufficient to record here that the Romans used hoists at the Colosseum for lifting the animals and gladiators into the amphitheatre, and also to lift heavy building materials for their temples etc. These hoists were in the form of a pulley wheel and rope wound round a geared capstan (Figure 11.1*a*).

The Industrial Revolution introduced water and steam power to power hoists; the most primitive form reserved for mine shafts was termed a 'man engine'. This comprised a single pole of connected timbers with platforms at regular intervals (Figure 11.1*b*). The up and down action was operated by a steam piston engine with the miners having to adroitly jump on and off the fixed platforms at the side of the shaft. Conventional elevators that used passenger cages and guide cables were water powered in those days. Such patterns were in common use until the 1870s and relied upon hydraulic rams to raise and lower the platform, not unlike 'Oildraulic' powered machinery today.

The revolutionary development of rack and pinion safety locks coupled with steam-powered machinery entirely changed lift engineering with the following dates as marker points in the new technology.

1853   Elisher Graves Otis demonstrated the safety lift by cutting suspension cable at the New York Crystal Palace Exhibition while a passenger on his own machine.

Figure 11.1a Medieval cathedral hoists (by kind permission of Otis Elevator plc)

1857   First Otis passenger lifts fitted in a Broadway store, New York.

1859   First Otis steam-powered lift.

1865   First Edoux hydraulic lift for the building trade.

1880   First Siemens electric lift.

1889   Otis electric lifts for the ascent to the second platform at the Eiffel Tower.[2]

1890   Paris International Exhibition. Moving pavements and escalators demonstrated for the first time. Escalators were patented by Otis and the word registered.

The movement pattern achieved by lifts totally changed the way tall buildings could be contrived. Dreams like the 'mile high' skyscraper of Frank Lloyd Wright

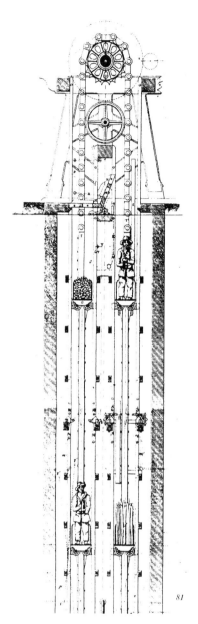

Figure 11.1b 'Man Engine' as used in Cornish tin mines (by kind permission of Otis Elevator plc)

have still to be built but the high rise architecture that distinguishes the twentieth and twenty-first centuries from previous history would never have occurred without the pioneering work of lift engineers in the nineteenth century (Figure 11.1c). The escalator and travelator first demonstrated at the Paris Exhibition in 1900

Figure 11.1c Lift cage in the Bradbury Building, Los Angeles, 1893, Architect: George M. Wyman (see also Figure 3.23)

have in turn transformed the handling of crowds in vast multi-storey spaces.

11.3 Lifts today

The basic types of lift can be defined by operating mode, each having its ideal application. Governing factors are the required performance in speed and capacity as well as running costs.

11.3.1 Roped systems
The majority of installations depend upon roped operations with ratios of 1:1 or 2:1

according to pulley arrangements. The most economic working is obtained with the electric traction unit mounted above the lift shaft. Mounting the traction machinery at or below the lowest floor served will reduce the shaft overrun to about 1 500 mm and save the cost of a construction at roof level. However, there are much higher running costs and greater loading on the shaft due to head pulleys. The selection of basement machinery rooms usually arises due to difficulties with accommodating structures above top floor level in conversion work or where architectural considerations limit the skyline. However, the greatest range of capacity, travel and speed can be obtained with roped systems employing overhead traction units.

11.3.2 Hydraulic systems
These systems are derived from the nineteenth century but operate with electric motors and pressurized oil. The basic provision includes a telescopic hydraulic cylinder which is housed centrally below the car or on either side. The simplest arrangement is the central cylinder with a shaft drilled down into the subsoil. Alternatives involve single or double cylinders to one or both sides of the shaft. The advantages rest with the minimum loading on the building and with the fact that the machinery room can be at lowermost level and up to 15 m away from the shaft. The limitations are speed and duty loads, say 0.63 m per second for loads around 1 000 kg. They are ideal for low rise (up to six storey) with non-intensive use.

11.3.3 Scissors lifts
Mainly employed for goods handling between two floors.

11.3.4 Paternoster lifts

A design depending upon an endless chain with cabins ascending and descending continuously between winding gear. The origins are industrial, with circulating pallets within a multi-storey plant, and are also used for refuse bin circulation in flats. Paternoster lifts were popular, mainly in Germany, in the immediate post-war years for serving high rise offices and public buildings, with six or more pairs of cabins working side by side. Lack of safety stops in case of blockage by goods or by passengers falling across the open fronts had led to the replacement of 'paternoster' equipment. The designs did not inspire confidence quite apart from the risk of severing leg or neck. The passenger cabins rattled and were often finished in identical but scuffed material to ceiling, floor and wall, giving the impression to the uninitiated that the conveyance went round the winding wheel leaving any left standing upside down for the descent!

11.3.5 Design selection and core planning

Selection of a system and operation depends upon design studies that take into account building use and occupancy. A single lift will generally only be suitable for a modest commercial building of five storeys and then provide poor service, there being no back-up if the lift is out of order.

Lifts are commonly grouped in pairs, fours etc., and are better distributed either side of a lobby which does not double as a through passage. Lobbies should be twice the depth of the car (Figure 11.2*a*). Modern control methods can maximize efficiency with collective calls either downwards or upwards or in both directions for the single lift or with groups, and can be programmed to resolve peak traffic movements, morning and evening.

Car and landing door configuration affect efficiency, the two panel, central opening pattern being the favoured solution. Four panel designs are needed for wider, larger cars. Asymmetric plans are more space-effective but slower in operation. The concluding illustration Figure 11.2*b* demonstrates the restrictions placed upon core planning with a high rise commercial building. The typical floor print in the AT&T headquarters, New York, reveals the 'racetrack' layout around the central core, with the lift lobby serving two rows of cars, and the separation of service lifts. The space of the lobby is dictated by fire regulations and also by the space needed for the machinery room at roof level. If residential floors exist, these have bypass shafts and separate entries at street level. In developments of 50 or more storeys it is common for lift operations to be staggered, for example, the lower group to serve up to level 25, the upper group to run level 1 to 25 non-stop and then stopping for the remainder, whilst a pair of cars might run non-stop to the penthouse suite.

11.4 Escalators

Today, escalators are used wherever a large number of people have to be moved at one time – shopping precincts, underground stations etc. In theatres they are particularly useful because before the performance they can be directed up to the auditorium and at the end they can take the audience down to street level.

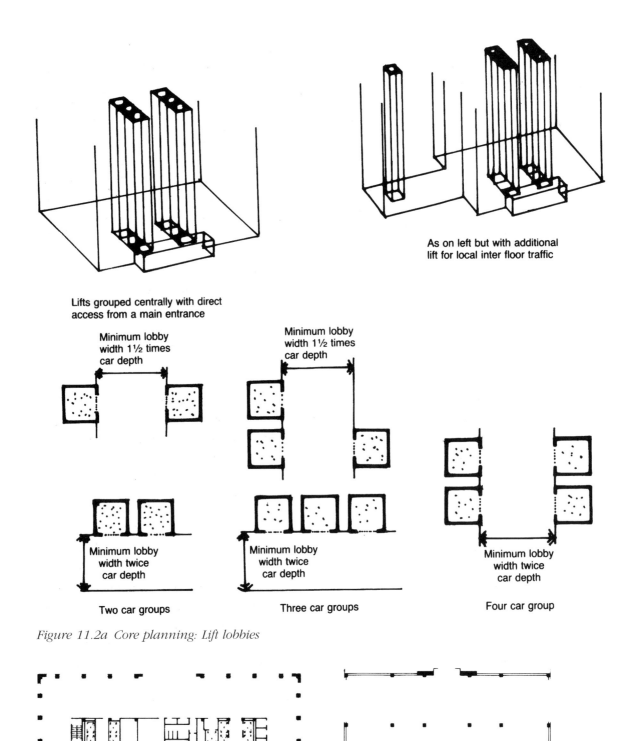

As on left but with additional
lift for local inter floor traffic

Lifts grouped centrally with direct
access from a main entrance

Minimum lobby
width 1½ times
car depth

Minimum lobby
width 1½ times
car depth

Minimum lobby
width twice
car depth

Minimum lobby
width twice
car depth

Minimum lobby
width twice
car depth

Two car groups

Three car groups

Four car group

Figure 11.2a Core planning: Lift lobbies

Figure 11.2b Lift core planning, flexibility in planning office space

Lifts take too long when a large number of people have to be moved at one time, as witnessed at the National Theatre. Stairs are disliked, particularly by the disabled, or as we become more and more lazy or elderly, and add to the difficulty of walking in unsuitable shoes when dressed up to go to the theatre.

One of the earliest large-scale applications were those installed by Otis for the Bakerloo and Piccadilly lines in the early 1900s. The familiar wood panelled designs with slatted wooden treads have only recently been removed following the terrible fire at Kings Cross. The original 'moving stairs' were the pride and joy of Frank Pick, the innovative manager of London Transport from 1907 onwards,[3] but the continual oiling and accumulation of dirt, together with drying out of the timber, made them a fire hazard. The pattern was copied in pre-war Moscow but the speeds increased from 0.75 to 1 m per second.

The early applications were in department stores, although the public were wary of the new invention even when geared down to 0.5 m per second. Otis were obliged to engage a wooden-legged naval officer in uniform to go up and down the newly installed escalators of Gimbel's store in Philadelphia, circa 1901. Those same 'moving stairs' had been demonstrated in the Paris Exhibition the previous year. The wooden-legged officer did further service as escalator attendant when installations were made in Paris, New York and finally London, at Harrods' store. Alternative moving stair designs were developed as 'corkscrew' forms, that were apparently installed at Holloway Road Station on the Piccadilly line but removed due to continuous break down.

The 1930s Harrods escalators elevated the new concept of moving stairs to an artistic form. Working models (Figure 11.3a) were made to show the Board the dramatic idea of the new escalator hall serving all floors of the department store. The finishes in polished brass provided a light reflective surface for both day and evening enjoyment, the 'portal wall' which led to the shopping floors having varied decor identifying the levels (Figure 11.3b). Regrettably the whole interior has been ripped out.

Reversible escalators were made for the underground and have a useful role in conference facilities or theatres where reverse flow is needed for intervals or at the end of a performance. A significant example is the London Theatre (mid-1960s) by Sean Kenny. Jeremy Dixon's first design for the London Opera House extension showed a grand sweeping staircase to rival the Garnier Paris Opera, but in the scheme built in 1999 a more practical escalator rises through the grand Floral Hall.

The acceptance of escalators as a normal conveyance has made immeasurable changes to the way building entries are laid out. The nineteenth-century idea of the spacious ground floor radiating towards grand stairs leading aloft is replaced by a multi-level vestibule. In these spaces the prime area may be below or at first floor enabling secondary and service functions to be tucked away. The elevation to first or second floor is a common solution in commercial designs, for example hotels and offices, where the ground floor may have premium value for retailing as well as finding space for vehicle ramps and for the 'porte cochère'. The ideas can be traced to pre-war designs: a truly seminal example is the first floor

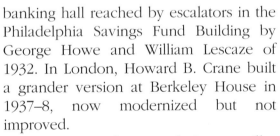

Figure 11.3a Escalator design: Concept model for Harrods' escalators, late 1930s (courtesy of Mr M. Al Fayed, Chairman of Harrods Ltd)

Figure 11.3b Interior of escalator hall, Harrods, finished in polished brass, Architect: Louis D. Blanc (courtesy of Mr M. Al Fayed, Chairman of Harrods Ltd)

banking hall reached by escalators in the Philadelphia Savings Fund Building by George Howe and William Lescaze of 1932. In London, Howard B. Crane built a grander version at Berkeley House in 1937–8, now modernized but not improved.

Two current Chicago solutions are illustrated which celebrate escalators to the virtual exclusion of lifts and stairs as the first impression upon entry. A splendid example is Water Tower Place (refer back to Figures 3.19*a* and 3.19*b*). This hotel and shopping mall atrium is entered at first floor via a special sequence, filled with a cascade of planters and water placed between metallic escalators (Figure 11.3*c*). The office towers of 311 South Waker Drive have a complex podium at second floor level

approached by escalator halls of Cecil B De Mille proportions. These in turn embrace a horseshoe run of food outlets and shops, together with a sunken conservatory (Figure 11.3*d*). All these elements effectively suppress the working core of lifts and service stairs which serve 50 or more storeys of offices above the podium to a lobby space of no significance.

11.5 Construction

Elevator construction is essentially a trussed beam to support the loop of stair-chain and treads with winding gear top and bottom. Recent changes have brought about transparent balustrades, while some

Figure 11.3c Escalator design: First stage entry to mall at Water Tower Place, Chicago, 1976, Architects: Loebl, Schlossman, Bennett and Partners

designs such as the installation at the Lloyd's Building, London, have the working mechanisms exposed to view within a glass-sided truss (Figure 11.4). Travelators are similar but lengths over 10 m will need supports at floor edges. There are limitations too on the rise of 6 m with inclines of 10° and 12° at speeds of 0.5 and 0.65 m per second respectively. Horizontal or near horizontal runs can be manufactured up to 120 m with inclines between 0° and 6° at speeds of 0.65–0.75 m per second. Footspace is needed for both types of equipment to house machinery around 2.5 m horizontally beyond the sloping part of the truss frame.

Figure 11.3d Escalator design: Main entry to 311 South Waker Drive, Chicago, with escalators and conservatory hall, 1990, Architects: Kohn Pederson Fox with Harwood K. Smith

11.6.2 The glass lift enclosure.
11.6.3 The multiple core of lift and/or elevator.
11.6.4 Travelator.

11.6 Design of lifts

In this review of related designs that exhibit new trends in the roles of elevators, escalators and travelators, the material is subdivided into design themes and studies in the following groups.

11.6.1 The metal cage, glass cabins and wall climbers.

11.6.1 The metal cage, glass cabins and wall climbers

The key reference point is the atrium in the Bradbury Building, referring back to Figures 11.1c and 3.23, where the bronze caged lift car rises in the open to the office balconies. Frank Lloyd Wright made an attractive allusion to a 'bird cage' theme in the lifts designed for the Johnson Building, Racine (Figure 11.5a).

Figure 11.4 Lifts and escalators assuming greater importance – interior of Lloyd's Building, London, 1986 (Richard Rogers Partnership)

Here, the circular cages run within an open framework through two storeys and are placed to give overall views of the celebrated workspace with the mushroom columns. It is part of the sense of openness that the directors' rooms have clear glass between their working areas and the general office.

The ultimate design of lifts is the wall climber whereby the lift cage rises on guides without an enclosed well. These were introduced by John Portman in the United States, mainly for the Hyatt Regency Hotels (refer back to Figure 3.8c and 3.10b). When placed externally, the view over the roofs as one rises adds to the general excitement (Figure 11.5b).

11.6.2 The glass lift enclosure

The Asplund-designed glass enclosure for the lift at the Gothenburg Courthouse takes minimalist ideas to their furthest extreme with a transparent cabin ascending within the open space to the balconies on first and second floor. The siting is placed at the critical junction between the main entrance and the base to the formal stairs rising to the first floor courts. Reference back to Figure 2.7a reveals the way the balance is struck between the formality of the judges and the modernity of the lift. This design is taken one stage further by Richard Rogers Partnership at 88 Wood Street (Figure 13.3) where two sides of the lift shaft are external walls which give great interest to passers-by at street level. The lift itself is an elegant glass cabin, including walls, door, floor and ceiling.

The next example is concerned with the detailing of the glass cabin and screening to the pair of hydraulic lifts which connect the basement, ground and mezzanine floors in the Sainsbury Arts Centre, Norwich, completed in 1977 by Foster and Partners. The first sketches by Norman Foster indicated glass walls wrapped round a minimal steel frame, with a grilled ceiling to cope with maintenance access and the housing for door mechanisms. The final details of the toughened glass enclosure to both the shaft and lift cars minimize their visual intrusion into the gallery. Using hydraulic rams means that the drive machinery is concealed at basement level. The precision jigging and high quality welding in the lift cars was a result of involving a car maker with the fabrication. Steel and aluminum for the moving parts are enamelled

Figure 11.5a The 'bird cages' designed for screens and cars at the Johnson Building, Racine, 1936, Architect: Frank Lloyd Wright

Figure 11.5b External wall-climber lifts, Channel 4, 1994 (Richard Rogers Partnership)

white while the static elements are aluminium or plated steel to match the metal finishes at mezzanine level. Figure 11.5c details the lift car as manufactured and the view in Figure 11.5d places the design within the context of the gallery space.

Compliance with safety requirements can often change a remarkable experience to one that is mediocre. The polished cages that graced Selfridges (1916) in times past now reside in the London Museum (Figure 11.5e) while the replacements are not worth recording.

The notable exception from our own time are the lifts placed in the open space encompassed by Le Grand Arche, Paris. The change in siting from internal to external has made a masterpiece of the composition (Figures 11.5f and 11.5g). The asymmetry and grand modelling provide a sense of surprise; they captivate the eye from a distance and fulfil the visual qualities needed when close up to an overscaled building. The 'cat's cradle' of cables contrasts with the panel grid façade. The movement through space to the exhibition hall above is an experience that rivals that obtained from the Otis route to the second platform of the Eiffel Tower.

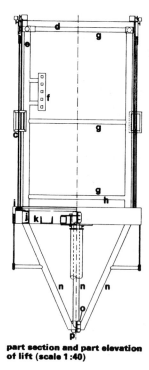

**part section and part elevation
of lift (scale 1:40)**

*Figure 11.5c Section detail of glass and steel
framing to lifts at the Sainsbury Arts Centre,
Norwich, 1977, Architect: Foster and Partners*

11.6.3 The multiple core of stair, lift and/or elevator

This selection has been culled from two pairs of buildings, each having a particular approach to the movement of people. The individual worlds have a distinguished pedigree, each representing a culminating point in design development with lifts and/or escalators by Foster and Partners[4] and Richard Rogers Partnership.[5]

The Willis Faber and Dumas Building has a superb elemental plan with the twin escalators serving the central bay of the layout. The mandatory cores with lifts and stairs are distributed four square within the remaining areas. The ascending escalators through the central bay open the departments to view floor by floor to reach the naturally-lit penthouse (Figure 11.6a).

Figure 11.5d View of glass and steel framing within the context of gallery space, Sainsbury Arts Centre

Figure 11.5e Beaux-Arts elegance: the bronze cages and decoration at Selfridges' store (1916) now in the London Museum. Architect: Daniel Burnham and others

Figure 11.5f The lifts that grace Le Grand Arche, Paris, 1990, Architect: Johann Otto von Sprekelsen

Figure 11.5g Detail view of lift construction, Le Grand Arche

Figure 11.6a Willis Faber & Dumas office building, Ipswich, 1975, Architects: Foster and Partners. Interior view of escalators within central bay of plan

The Hong Kong and Shanghai Bank stretches the ascending spaces of Willis Faber into a vertical stack of floors that rise 40 storeys (refer to Figures 2.19*a–c*). The subdivision of a banking headquarters, unlike insurance, falls into three zones: the public domain of street and trading floors, the working areas and the zones where privacy and security are most important. The public domain is served by a pair of escalators from the plaza to the main public floor (Level 3). A further pair climb to the secondary banking level (Level 5). Inter-floor escalators cope with office traffic from Level 10

through to 35. The lifts have access to all floors and are distributed to both sides of the floor spaces served. Four double-height zones exist within the tower connected by high-speed lifts to form secondary entrances. These also provide the refuge areas required by the Fire Regulations in Hong Kong. A further advantage is the division of the façade. The integration of movement spaces with the structure is helped by logical disposal of stairs and lifts to the edges of the spaces served.

The Centre Pompidou in Paris arose from an international competition in 1971, when the design by Piano and Rogers was selected as the prize winner. The main entrance to the Centre Pompidou is on the west side towards

Place Beaubourg from the sunken level of the square. The entry to the Centre follows an anticlockwise pattern with internal escalators taking visitors to the upper mezzanine level where there are galleries and circulation space. These in turn lead round to the most popular feature, the external escalator promenade to the prin-cipal gallery and museum space at third, fourth and fifth floors (Figure 11.6b). For many visitors the sheer delight of the building is the method of circulation through the transparent escalator 'tubes' (Figure 11.6c). The very popularity of the exhibitions has raised the issue of increasing the number of 'tubes'. Crowd

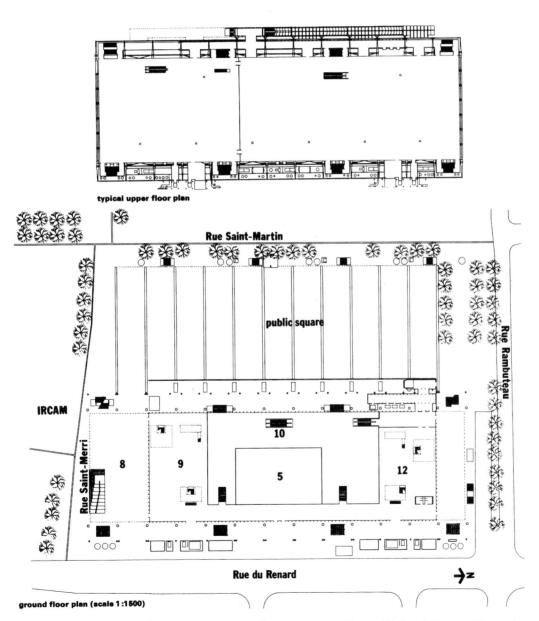

Figure 11.6b Centre Pompidou, Paris, 1977, Architects: Renzo Piano, Richard Rogers. Plans at street level and sixth floor gallery level.

Figure 11.6c View of escalators externally, Centre Pompidou (courtesy of Martin Charles)

control today means queues. The spacious entries have had to absorb the paraphernalia of barriers and security checks. Re-ordering the entry arrangements and an external canopy to protect the waiting crowds would solve the present bottleneck when popular events occur. However, once entered upon 'Le grand escalier mouvant' all is forgiven: the movement, the excitement of the structure sliding past and the vision of Paris is spectacular. It is little wonder that Centre Pompidou has more visitors that Gustaf Eiffel's famous tower.

Some years ago a pair of 1:50 models stood side by side in the lobby of Rogers' office: the Centre Pompidou next to the Lloyd's Building. The two designs are ten years apart but represent a great similarity in the separation of building roles. Both have servant spaces clustered to the edges of the main activity areas; those master spaces enjoy clear volumes to provide total freedom in use. The Lloyd's Building has a range of sophisticated options, a trading space that can envelop the whole central volume, commercial offices that might diminish or grow again according to market forces and finally the headquarters' back-up in the basement and penthouse suites. The servicing of Pompidou is handled like an industrial plant, or airport or railway station. It is sturdy and robust like street furniture. Lloyd's could be described as a 'machine for working in'. The wall-climber lifts and stair pods although external in form are part of the interior experience (Figure 11.7a) and finished to Savile Row standard. The detailing of the lifts with stainless steel and glass are for 'external' wall climbers. The increased specification matches the exterior climate. The critical zone between car and landing gate received special attention. A new form of retractable weatherproof seal was developed by the Express Lift Company. The floors of the cars were also placed in isolation to the chassis to overcome wind turbulence. The actual enclosure was a simple toughened glass box made with silicone bonding. The concept, though extravagent, provides exciting views that equal those from the prominent 'escalier mouvant' at Pompidou. The stair pods are clad in stainless steel to conform to the dog-leg profile; internally the landings and stair waists are concrete with raised landings and tread/riser components in extruded aluminium (Figure 11.7b for

constructional detail). The real triumph of Lloyd's is the flexible interior volume bridged by crossover escalators that enable the users to trade throughout the core of the Lloyd's vertical room. The spatial arrangement is not obvious at first impact since the escalator bridges run the shortest direction, unlike the public entry to the Hong Kong and Shanghai Bank.

11.6.4 Travelators

The major application of travelators occurs in airports but few of these experiences are memorable. Gatwick certainly provides a convenient ride through the neutral scenery bequeathed by BAA (Figure 11.8a). The dramatic system adopted by Auketts at Manchester leads the travellers through a space-age glass and aluminium tube connecting the rail terminal to the airport (Figure 11.8b). Other devices in Europe include travelator tunnels that dip and climb to prevent boredom as at Charles de Gaulle, Paris. It is this airport that placed satellite escalators within a globe-like sphere that shuttles travellers off to their various departures (Figure 11.8c). The aesthetic delights within 'the shape of things to come' are not matched by creature comforts. It does seem that the future of 'Travelatorscape' should provide enhancing experiences in line with the moving girdle at O'Hare Airport, Chicago, which runs with suitable breaks through a typical American mall – a route that is lined like a modern-day Aladdin's cave with drink and food outlets, fortune tellers, shoe shiners and every conceivable service in washrooms.

The serrated tread has enabled airport and supermarket trolleys to be conveyed

Figure 11.7a Lloyd's Building, London, 1986, Architects: Richard Rogers Partnership. External view of staircase towers

safely on inclines up to 10°: the most stylish example is the connecting travelators within the glazed foyer designed by Grimshaw for Sainsbury at Camden Town (Figure 11.8*d*).

The same designer has utilized travelators to move visitors through the British Pavilion at the Seville Expo. The installation permits a regular movement of people to save holdups and to reduce queuing time. The up and down sequence occurs along the long frontages of the open plan and enables the exhibition

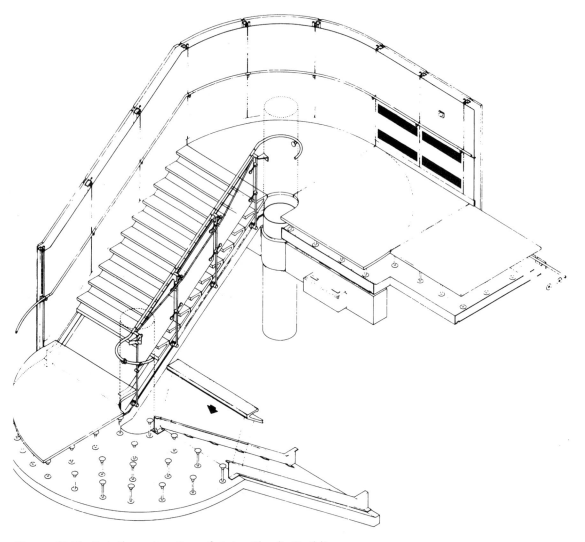

Figure 11.7b Detail construction of stairs, Lloyd's Building

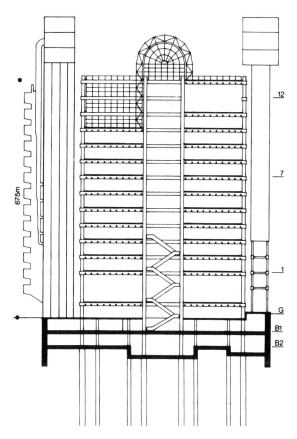

Figure 11.7c Section detail, Lloyd's Building

spaces to be fully enjoyed. The internal structure of the Pavilion has six bays of structural columns. These are grouped at three positions to maximize the space; the travelator trusses span between support arms jettied off the columns (Figure 11.8*e*).

11.7 Ramps and chair lifts for the disabled

11.7.1 Public buildings

Under the revised Building Regulations provision has to be made for the physically impaired and those in wheelchairs to negotiate changes of level in public buildings. It is easy to plan for the disabled in new buildings but work has to be undertaken to all existing buildings. This can be carried out in three ways.

- *Ramps.* This is the easiest if space is available adjacent to the steps. The pitch can be a maximum of 1 in 12 provided it does not exceed 5 m in length, or 1 in 15 over 10 m.
- *Hoists.* For differences of height where a conventional lift is not required, small hydraulic hoists are produced, whereby a wheelchair is wheeled onto a platform, the guards closed behind and the platform raised to the required height for the chair to be pushed forward. An excellent design is at the Louvre in Paris (Figure 11.9*a*).
- *Stairlifts.* Stannah Stairlifts produce chairs which run on guides up the side of the stairs. This means a wheelchair user has to get out of the chair and sit on the seat and is then carried to the top (Figure 11.9*b*). For very wide stairs the stairlift has been adapted to provide a platform to take a wheelchair (Figure 11.9*c*).
- *Platform lifts.* Small single-person electric lifts are now available from Gartec, which do not require a separate lift shaft or machine room, just a 50 mm pit. The overall size is 1 600 × 1 375 mm with a rise up to 9 m with a 400 kg load.

11.7.2 Domestic lifts

- *Chair lifts.* These can be provided to straight flights and can also be designed to turn right-angles so that the passenger can get off onto a flat surface rather than the top step.

Figure 11.8a Travelator foyer, Gatwick Airport, 1980, Architects: YRM

Figure 11.8b Manchester Airport's new 240 m travelator (courtesy of Paul Miller)

Figure 11.8c Satellite globe, Charles de Gaulle Airport, 1970 (courtesy of the Architectural Association)

Figure 11.8e Travelators within the British Pavilion, Seville, 1992, Architect: Nicholas Grimshaw and Partners

Figure 11.8d Trolley on travelator at Sainsbury's Camden Town, 1989, Architect: Nicholas Grimshaw and Partners

Figure 11.9a Hoist at the Louvre

Figure 11.9c Stair lift for wheelchair

- *Hoists.* Home hoists to take a wheel-chair from ground to first floor are now possible. A hole is made in the first floor, guides are bolted to an external wall and a small open cabinet, approximately 1 200 mm high with platform, takes the passenger up or down. It is driven electrically (Figure 11.9*d*). The guides are unobstrusive and when the platform is in its raised position the underside is flush with the ceiling, so that even when situated in a living room it is acceptable.

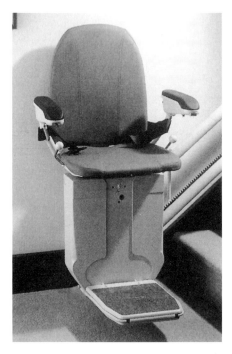

Figure 11.9b Stannah Stair chair lift

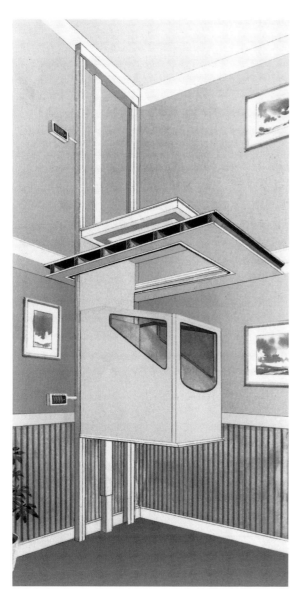

Figure 11.9d Domestic hoist for two floors

References

1 *Going Up. An informal history of the elevator from the Pyramids to the present*, Jean Gavois, Otis Elevator Company, 1983.

2 *The Eiffel Tower*, Joseph Harriss, Elek Books, 1975.

3 *A Biography of Frank Pick*, Christian Barman, David and Charles, 1979. Pick's authoritative regime included personal inspections of stations and escalators at 2.00 a.m. in the morning!

4 For further reading on the two Foster designs selected refer to Foster and Partners, *Building and Projects*, Volumes 2 and 3.

5 For further reading on Rogers' design: 'Pompidou', *Architectural Review*, May 1977. 'Lloyd's Building', *Architectural Review*, October 1986. Refer also to *Richard Rogers. A biography*, Bryan Appleyard, Faber & Faber, 1986.

12 International case studies

The intention of the last two chapters is to present some outstanding examples of stairs, escalators and lifts designed in the last 15 years. A few of the studies were included in the original book, but these, as in the case of the Pyramid in Le Grand Louvre, Paris, are exceptional and should never be omitted from any book on the subject of stairs.

Sculptural forms applied to stairs give the building interest and frequently it is

Figure 12b Penguin Pool, London Zoo, Architect: Lubetkin, Drake and Tecton

Figure 12a Vitra International Furniture Museum at Wein on Rhein, Architect: Frank Gehry

Figure 12c Sculpture by Louise Bourgeis for Tate Modern opening 2000

the suggestion of the stair behind, as expressed in the elevation, that is so intriguing. A good example of this is the Vitra International Furniture Museum at Weil am Rhein by Frank Gehry. Perhaps the greatest sculptural ramp of all was not for humans but for penguins at the London Zoo, by Lubetkin, Drake and Tecton. When the penguins are lined up waiting for food, they compare well with the gentlemen in black tie and tails of the musical extravaganza of the 1930s film (refer to Figure 2.29). Also worthy of note are the three sculptures by Louise Bourgeois exhibited at the opening of the New Tate Museum in 2000 where staircases swirl round the central columns to enable the viewer to climb up to the top platforms to view the mirrors at close quarters.

Case Study 12.1 The Guggenheim Museum, Bilbao (1997)

Architect: Frank Gehry

The Guggenheim Museum is perhaps the most outstanding building of the twentieth century and appropriate that it should be completed at the century's very end. The invention of the computer helped to provide the very complicated drawings for its construction. It is very fitting that it should have been built in Spain where Gaudi produced many intriguing free-shaped buildings and would no doubt have been fascinated by the virtuosity of the computer.

The interior stairs of the Guggenheim are utilitarian, but there are three very imposing stairs externally. First, a flight which starts at the free-standing tower and widens as its descends to the promenade which separates the lake between the building and the river. At the end of the promenade a further route leads to another perspective flight which narrows to the doors of the restaurant. Finally on the other side of the building another stair

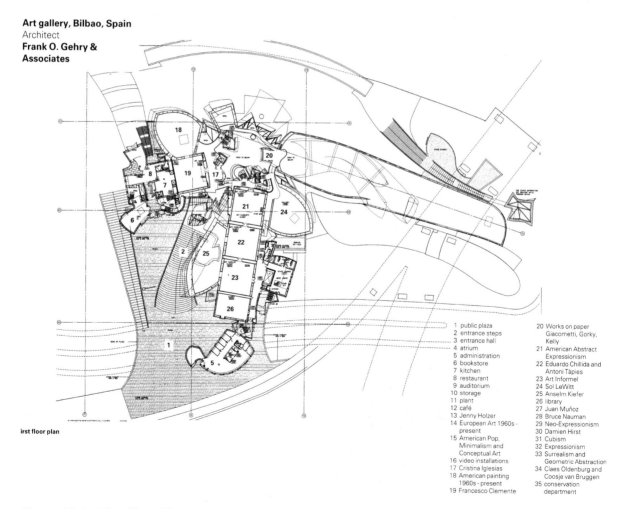

Art gallery, Bilbao, Spain
Architect
Frank O. Gehry & Associates

irst floor plan

1 public plaza	20 Works on paper
2 entrance steps	Giacometti, Gorky,
3 entrance hall	Kelly
4 atrium	21 American Abstract
5 administration	Expressionism
6 bookstore	22 Eduardo Chillida and
7 kitchen	Antoni Tàpies
8 restaurant	23 Art Informel
9 auditorium	24 Sol LeWitt
10 storage	25 Anselm Kiefer
11 plant	26 library
12 café	27 Juan Muñoz
13 Jenny Holzer	28 Bruce Nauman
14 European Art 1960s -	29 Neo-Expressionism
present	30 Damien Hirst
15 American Pop,	31 Cubism
Minimalism and	32 Expressionism
Conceptual Art	33 Surrealism and
16 video installations	Geometric Abstraction
17 Cristina Iglesias	34 Claes Oldenburg and
18 American painting	Coosje van Bruggen
1960s - present	35 conservation
19 Francesco Clemente	department

Figure 12.1a First Floor Plan

Figure 12.1b River front

Figure 12.1c Steps leading to tower

sweeps down to the main entrance of the gallery. All these steps are planned to take the large numbers of visitors that flock to the museum.

Case Study 12.2 The Reichstag, Berlin (1998)

Architects: Foster and Partners

The refurbishment of the derelict German parliament building has enabled Foster and Partners to rebuild the domes as a giant viewing bubble. The visitor is taken directly by lift to the main roof terrace where the dome is entered; the ascent to the top is via a ramp cantilevered from the steel ribs of the structure. As one rises, the panoramic views over the city, and in par-ticular the Chancellery and Brandenburg Gate, grow more and more spectacular. From the platform at the top one looks down through the internal mirrored glass lantern to the debating chamber below. This lantern also serves to reflect daylight into the building. Once rested, the visitor returns by a second ramp, the down ramp.

The view from the ground when looking up is of little ant-like people circumnavigating the dome. The effect is even greater at dusk when the colours from the sky show the ramps and figures in silhouette.

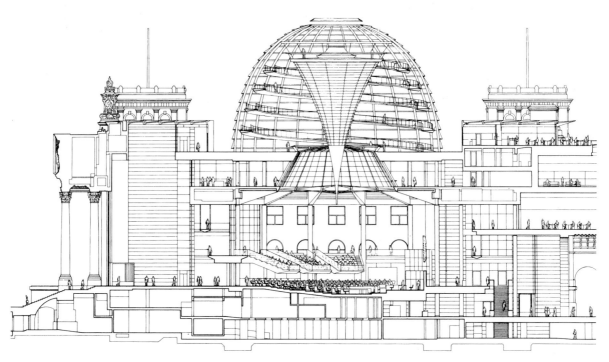

Figure 12.2a Section (Architecture Today, May 1999)

Figure 12.2b Ramp at dusk

Figure 12.2c Detail of ramp support

Case Study 12.3 Jewish Museum, Berlin (1999)

Architect: Daniel Libeskind

The Jewish Museum is a symbolic build-ing, designed to represent the history of the Jews and the Holocaust. The stair is likewise symbolic as it rises from the basement entrance of the old Berlin Museum up between two walls with doors off each landing to the various exhibition spaces on each floor. As the visitor rises towards the light with a feel-ing of hope, the stair terminates abruptly and a few steps above the top the path is terminated by a blank wall. Turning back, the frustration of entrapment is created by the criss-cross of beams that bar the way. There was no escape from the concentration camp.

Figure 12.3a Looking up the stair

Figure 12.3b Looking back

Case Study 12.4 Le Grand Louvre, Paris (1989)

Architects: Pei, Cobb, Freed and Partners

The Grand Projects in Paris have led to a number of outstanding designs: none more controversial or spectacular than the glazed pyramid that forms the portal to the new sunken entrance of the Louvre Museum. Set in the centre of this historic palace which houses one of the world's greatest art galleries, this modern edifice connects the three pavilions in an elegant foyer. The popularity, as with Centre Pompidou, has produced the long queues of crowd control in the old courtyard. However, once the security check is passed, the public freely descend into the new vestibule. The descent can be made by hydraulic platform or else by a gracious concrete spiral which curls around the lift drum. The mechanics of the design are sublime, with the open platform elevated on a stainless cylinder which descends into the ground.

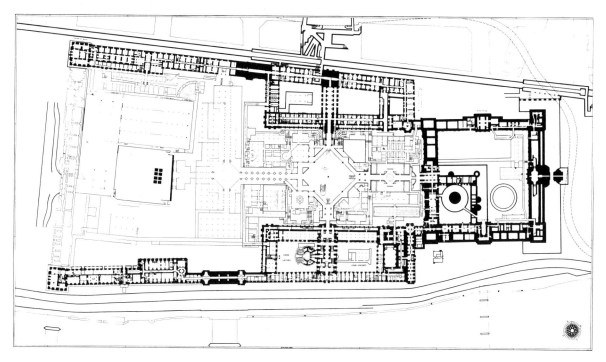

Figure 12.4a Layout plan at lower vestibule level

Figure 12.4b General view of stair and platform of hydraulic lift

Figure 12.4c Stair with lift lowered

Case Study 12.5 State of Illinois Center, Chicago (1985)

Architect: Helmut Jahn and Partners

The round atrium is fully glazed externally and penetrates the total height of the offices. A cluster of wall-climber lifts are the main focus within the inner space of the atrium and relate to circular galleries floor by floor. Accommodation and escape stairs run in a zig zag pattern down the balcony face and contribute an expression of activity and movement within the 16 storey volume. The lower-most floors relate to a food hall and to the subway system. It is one of the most remarkable public buildings in the United States and particularly in the way that changing technology permits lifts and stairs to assume significance within an open interior.

Figure 12.5a General floor plan

Figure 12.5b Detail view of stairs

Figure 12.5c General view of atrium drum with wall-climber lifts and stairs

Case Study 12.6 Dresdner Bank, Pariser Platz, Berlin

Architects: GMP Von Gerkan, Marg and Partner

This building is very similar in plan to the State of Illinois Center, a large circular atrium, lit from above. The offices are entered off a circular gallery on each floor. These are accessed by a helical stair with lift on either side.

The stair consists of dark grey steel strings to which metal brackets are welded; the brackets support circular glass pads on which the translucent glass treads rest. The galleries are of similar construction and are enlivened and become luminous from lamps at the edges which glow in their own right.

Figure 12.6b View of stair

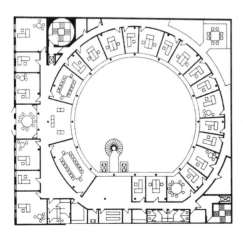

Figure 12.6a General floor plan (Architectural Review, January 1999)

Figure 12.6c Detail of tread support

Case Study 12.7 Gregory-Ingraham House, San Francisco, California

Architects: Jeremy Kotas and Skip Shaffer

A circular timber stair ascends through the house up to the double-height living room. Here the stairs change character as they rise with steel treads cantilevered precariously off the living room wall to the library balcony, thence traversing a steel gangplank to the bedroom.

The stair forms the central feature of the whole complex.

Figure 12.7 View of steel cantilevered stair from living room to library gallery (courtesy of Arcaid

13 Case studies in the UK

Case Study 13.1 No. 1, Poultry, City of London (1998)

Architects: James Stirling, Michael Wilford and Associates Ltd

This is a very interesting cross between a stair and ramp. The site is triangular with the prow facing a main road junction

Figure 13.1b Site plan (Architecture Today, September 1998)

which is surrounded by the important buildings of the Bank of England (Soane), Midland Bank (Lutyens), the Mansion House (Dance the Elder), and St Mary Woolnoth (Hawksmoor). The

Figure 13.1a View looking up stairs

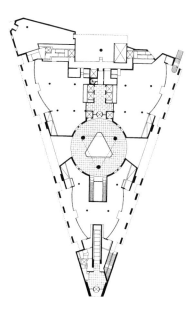

Figure 13.1c Floor plan (Architecture Today, September 1998)

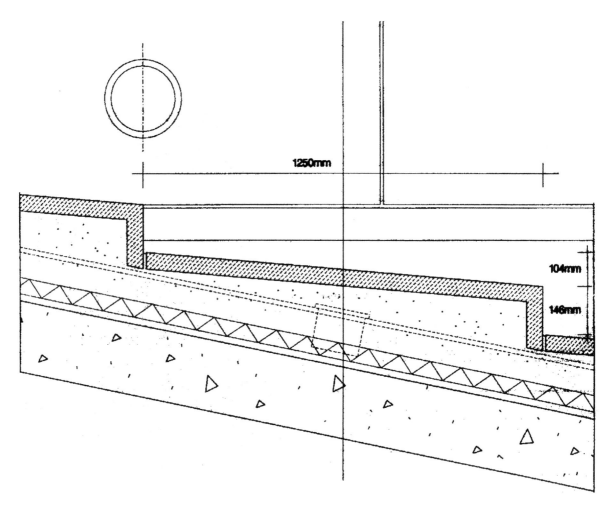

Figure 13.1d Detail of steps

revolving doors lead into a small reception area and thence to the ceremonial grand stair. As one looks up to the light, the central circular court, with its open atrium is revealed. The stair runs between two walls, with steps of 146 mm and the going 1 250 mm which rises as a ramp of 104 mm, giving a total rise of 250 mm and therefore a pitch of 1 in 5.

The slabs are kept about 300 mm short of each wall, the gap being a continuous ramp into which spot lights are set on the centre of each tread. Port lights are set into the vertical walls. A truly dramatic concept.

Case Study 13.2 National Portrait Gallery Extension, London (2000)

Architects: Jeremy Dixon and Edward Jones

The re-ordering of the National Portrait Gallery has opened up the vertical circulation to provide a fine internal space. A simple timber stair takes the visitor up to mezzanine and first floor, with a long escalator taking the weary up to the second floor. Escalators do not require landings after 15 steps and the rise can be greater, therefore the space required is far less than an ordinary flight of stairs.

Figure 13.2 Stair and escalator, entrance hall

Case Study 13.3 88 Wood Street, London EC2 (1990)

Architects: Richard Rogers Partnership

This is an impressive all-glass building situated on a prominent site at the junction of London Wall and Wood Street in the heart of the City of London. Through the glass box a fine lift and stair is the main feature. The dog-leg stair rises within a glass tube with bright yellow steelwork for the internal framework. This contrasts with the stainless steel cladding of the service nodes at the Lloyd's Building by the same architect. The stair has open metal trays supported on folded metal brackets; the treads and landings are covered with 5 mm black ribbed rubber surface with 25×52 mm natural anodized aluminium nosing.

It is the lifts, also with bright yellow stanchions, which are the most spectacular: completely glass framed, including floor, ceiling, sides and doors. Like wall-climber lifts, one can view all the mechanics, pulleys etc. from both the lift lobby and the pavement outside. Many years ago a curtain wall office block had to add a courtesy panel to the lower part of each window panel because the typists complained that passers-by could look up their skirts as they walked or drove past. Let us hope that trousers or tight skirts are worn to obviate any such problems as the lift rises above eye level.

Figure 13.3a View of lift

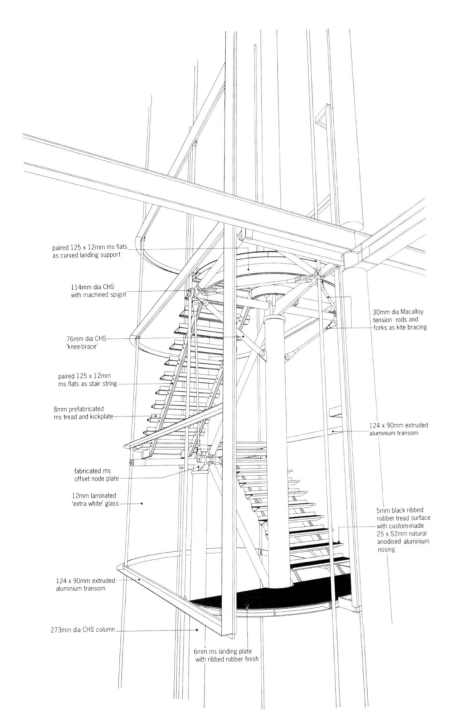

paired 125 x 12mm ms flats
as curved landing support

114mm dia CHS
with machined spigot

76mm dia CHS
'knee-brace'

paired 125 x 12mm
ms flats as stair string

8mm prefabricated
ms tread and kickplate

fabricated ms
offset node plate

12mm laminated
'extra white' glass

124 x 90mm extruded
aluminium transom

273mm dia CHS column

6mm ms landing plate
with ribbed rubber finish

30mm dia Macalloy
tension rods and
forks as kite bracing

124 x 90mm extruded
aluminium transom

5mm black ribbed
rubber tread surface
with custom-made
25 x 52mm natural
anodised aluminium
nosing

Figure 13.3b Perspective sketch of staircase construction (Architect's Journal)

Case Study 13.4 RAC Headquarters, Bristol (1989)

Architects: Nicholas Grimshaw and Partners

This is a very interesting building in terms of staircase planning. The three-sided, three-storey glass building has an internal three-sided atrium. Three flights of stairs, one from each side of the offices, descend to a large central platform or meeting place, where there is a choice of three further flights of stairs to each of the sides on the lower floor. A similar arrangement takes one down to the canteen and social facilities on the ground floor. Each flight is constructed of painted steel beams supporting steel treads. The whole structure, however, floats in the atrium. The

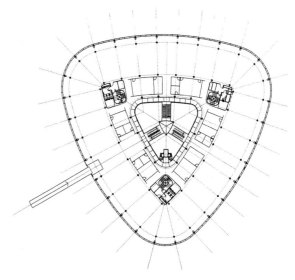

Figure 13.4b Floor plan

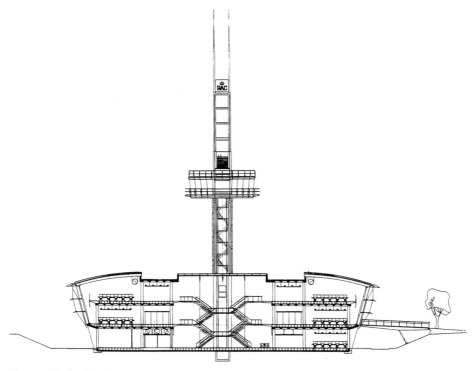

Figure 13.4a Section

Figure 13.4c Looking down to stair

platforms are hung by cables from the roof beams and they in turn support the stair strings. The internal space created is a work of art.

There are three escape stairs tucked into the three internal angles to comply with the Fire Regulations.

Case Study 13.5 Peckham Library, One Stop Shop (1999)

Architects: Alsop and Stormer

This is a small gem, a staircase taking one up to a private interview platform. The pod is a timber construction, faced with stained 1.5 mm ply tiles stapled to oriented strand board (OSB) outer skin. The staircase is a stringless folded plate structure of solid Douglas fir. Treads and risers were finger-jointed together in 50 mm wide strips and pressure glued with a hydraulic ram. The strips were then jointed and glued. The finish is clear stained. The handrail and balusters are formed with 12×50 mm ms flats bolted to risers with coach screws set in sockets.

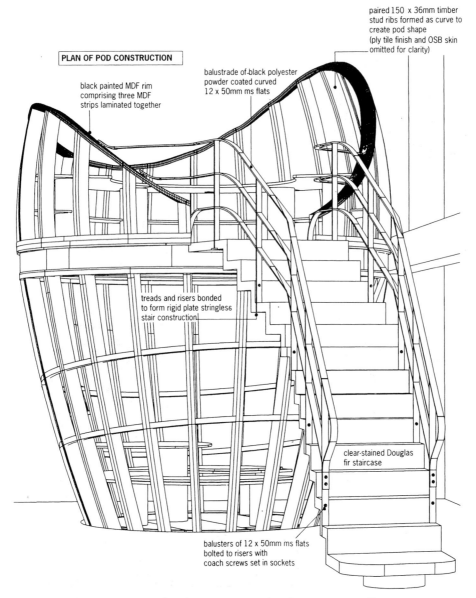

PLAN OF POD CONSTRUCTION

black painted MDF rim comprising three MDF strips laminated together

balustrade of black polyester powder coated curved 12 x 50mm ms flats

paired 150 x 36mm timber stud ribs formed as curve to create pod shape (ply tile finish and OSB skin omitted for clarity)

treads and risers bonded to form rigid plate stringless stair construction

clear-stained Douglas fir staircase

balusters of 12 x 50mm ms flats bolted to risers with coach screws set in sockets

Figure 13.5a Perspective of pod construction (Architect's Journal)

Figure 13.5b General view of stair

Figure 13.5c Detail view

Case Study 13.6 House at Chagford, Devon

Designer: Philip Watts

The client's brief for the renovation of this Victorian house was to open up the rather dark entrance hall and to make the space its focal point. The existing solid timber stair was removed and a dog-leg stair with glass treads on sculptured polished cast aluminium cantilever brackets was installed. The brackets were bolted through the adjacent brick wall. The glass treads are etched to give a non-slip surface. The balustrade consists of stainless steel newels with straining wires between. The handrails are capped with beech to the first two flights and white handrails to the upper flights. The final translucent creation allows for views through the stair to the French windows and garden beyond and glimpses of sky through the landing window above.

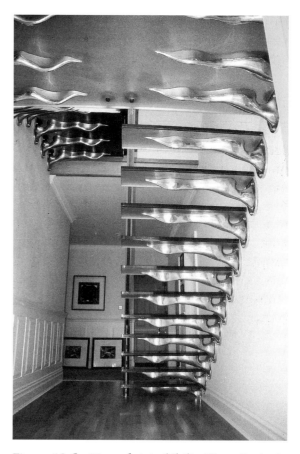

Figure 13.6a View of stair (Philip Watts Design)

Figure 13.6b Detail of cantilever brackets

Case Study 13.7 Liquid Nightclub, Gloucester

Designer: Philip Watts

This is a spiral stair made of cast aluminium very suitable for the decor of a nightclub. The whole concept is a decorative piece of sculpture. Inspiration comes from water forms, with puddle-like treads with a hand-textured edge, and a water-droplet 'grab hold' handrail twisting around the central column. Snake-like balustrades give an enticing effect combined with the strobe lighting of the venue.

Figure 13.7 General view of stair

Case Study 13.8 Private House, Clifton Terrace, Dublin

Architect: A & D Wejchert Architects

This is a beautiful light spiral stair, 1670 mm diameter, constructed from bright polished stainless steel and acrylic. From the main stainless steel column, cantilevered triangular tread frames are

Figure 13.8b Detail of top of stair (Spiral Staircase Systems)

Figure 13.8a General view of stair (Spiral Staircase Systems)

bolted. These are infilled with sheet acrylic with non-slip aluminium strips set into the top surface. A neat 'D' bracket, below the nosing, copes with the Building Regulations whereby there should be no gap greater than 100 mm between treads in domestic houses.

The handrail is a sinuous stainless steel circular tube. The balustrade is almost invisible, being moulded clear acrylic fixed to the end of the treads and slotted into the handrail.

Case Study 13.9 Churchill House, London

Architect: ORMS Architects

Not an elegant stair but constructionally interesting. The shallow mild steel stringers are kept to a minimum depth and are reinforced with stainless steel tension cables to form beams. The framing is completed with rods at each baluster which tie the strings together. The glass treads are supported on slips. The whole structure floats above the floor on brackets.

Figure 13.9a View looking up (Spiral Staircase Systems)

Figure 13.9b View from underside (Spiral Staircase Systems)

Case Studies 13.10–13.13 Jubilee Line Stations (1999)

The last case studies feature four of the new Jubilee Line underground stations. All these stations provide facilities for the disabled in wheelchairs with lifts taking the passengers directly from the platform to the street pavement level. Escalators rather than stairs take all passengers from the trains to the entrance.

Case Study 13.10 Stratford Station

Architects: Wilkinson Eyre Architects

Here the lift, escalator and stair meet adjacent to each other in a large modern concourse. The glass hydraulic lift takes wheelchair users and parents with children in pushchairs either up or down; a single escalator takes passengers up, this being preferred by the majority of the old or lazy, and a wide stair takes the surging crowds down quickly.

Figure 13.10 Stratford Station, Wilkinson Eyre Architects: lift, escalator and stairs

Case Study 13.11 Canary Wharf

Architects: Foster and Partners

Travel from the platform is up single escalators to a cathedral-like large concourse, a double-height space with exits at either end. Here a bank of four escalators, two up and two down, take travellers to a glazed shell canopy and the open air to a large pedestrian piazza. A lift up to the entrance is concealed adjacent to the escalators.

Figure 13.11 Canary Wharf Station, Foster and Partners

Case Study 13.12 Southwark Station

Architects: MacCormac, Jamieson, Pritchard

This is in complete contrast to Canary Wharf where, instead of the vast spaces created, the escalators are single and rise up in a tunnel-like structure. The tube is lit by spotlights set into the side walls and travellers rise to a blue-clad vestibule as if they are rising to a moonlit sky, lit by small spotlights looking like stars. This is a dramatic solution.

Figure 13.12 Southwark Station, MacCormac, Jamieson and Pritchard

Case Study 13.13 Westminster Station

Architects: Michael Hopkins and Partners

This is situated in the basement of the new parliamentary building with its foundations and services weaving their way through the spaces. It is a fantastic, dramatic space to be compared with the Piranesi drawing that introduced the book in Figure 1.2. Thus we have gone full circle to show that stairs are the design feature of a building that creates the greatest interest. At Westminster the escalators and stairs span vast distances and as one looks down it appears that ants are travelling through space.

Figure 13.13 Westminster Station, Michael Hopkins and Partners (courtesy of Dennis Gilbert)

Epilogue

It is sad to find that in more and more public buildings the grand staircase is being replaced by escalators. These are utilitarian as they have to rise from one point to another in a straight line. The wonderful curves of Garnier's stair at the Paris Opera House, which takes up such a large area of the vestibule but forms the great meeting space, becomes an escalator in the London Opera House extension. While writing this book, I stayed at Tours where Jean Nouvel built a fine new Conference Centre. I felt there might be a wonderful new stair here – but no, the inevitable escalator was used. Stairs will continue to be used in houses where there is no space for an escalator.

In Les Gallery Lafayette one of the great stairs has been removed to provide more merchandising area.

Today, many of the interesting stairs are spiral or helical, but let us hope that this book may help to stimulate the desire to produce more interesting designs and for the designer to think hard and not just provide the simplest solution. Just think of the imagination of Piranesi.

Index